The Professional Project Manager

The Professional Project Manager

How We Become True Professionals

Carsten H. Laugesen

BEP
BUSINESS EXPERT PRESS
Leader in applied, concise business books

The Professional Project Manager: How We Become True Professionals

First published in 2024 by
Business Expert Press, LLC
222 East 46th Street, New York, NY 10017
www.businessexpertpress.com

ISBN-13: 978-1-63742-569-5 (paperback)
ISBN-13: 978-1-63742-570-1 (e-book)

Business Expert Press Portfolio and Project Management Collection

First edition: 2024

10 9 8 7 6 5 4 3 2 1

Description

How do we become good project managers? What does it take to become a true professional?

This book gives depth to these crucial questions. It explains and illustrates the experiences and professional capacities we must acquire to become good at what we do. The entry point is project management, and this entry point is used to define what, in general, makes us become good professionals. The book shows that our professional capacity is so much more than our technical abilities and that becoming a true professional today is defined by three key factors:

- Our ability to accumulate relevant professional **reference points and contexts**
- Our ability to **juggle technical, people, power, and unforeseen professional agendas**
- Our ability to **memorize our experiences in useful mental models**

The world will end up having around 8 billion professionals, which means that more than 150,000 new professionals will enter the workforce *every day* for the next 75 years. This will dramatically change our professional context.

This book is for everyone who wants to **sharpen their professional skills and mental models to stay relevant.**

Keywords

project management; project manager; professional; accumulation of experiences; reference points; mental models

Contents

Testimonials

"I have had the privilege of working with Laugesen on some of his many projects, and in The Professional Project Manager, *I find he distils the wisdom and creativity he has learned and practiced in a lifetime of undertaking projects, professionally, one after the other. Quiet wisdom and gentle advice from an expert, enlivened by personal examples and lessons learned."*
—**Thammarat Kootatep, Professor, Asian Institute of Technology, Bangkok, Thailand**

"Navigating the transformation from novice to a conveyer of invaluable expertise is a nuanced expedition. In The Professional Project Manager, *Laugesen emerges as a sagacious guide on this odyssey. His method is grounded in experiential learning, interweaving anecdotes, stories, and lessons learned. Laugesen meticulously consolidates these insights into a compelling theoretical framework, resulting in a highly informative and enriching book for those aspiring to true professionalism in project management."*—**Hans Brix, Professor and Head of Department of Biology, Aarhus University, Denmark**

"An essential read for project managers, professionals and anyone who cares about improving performance. Becoming good at something is a lifelong never-ending task. I am certain this insightful and experience-based book will make you look at your professional skills in a fresh perspective."—**Dorah Modise, CEO, PRO Alliance, South Africa**

*"*The Professional Project Manager *is a gem of a book, persuasive and highly readable. I really enjoyed reviewing this book. I had a good laugh when I read that we are all useless in our first year of employment. Spot on. I also had a laugh when he states that Denmark's international development assistance to South Africa, which he oversaw for 3 years, were 'all non-priority sectors for the South African government'. His doomed writing on the wall story from Samara made me smile at first, then reflect on content. I enjoyed reading*

about his gradual transition from rural Plougstrup in Denmark to megacity Johannesburg. The personal narrative, life companionships and endeavours make the book engaging and a really good read. I found his description of the four pillars of power in Thailand insightful, and his reflections on foreign aid and bulldozing environmentalism thought provoking. I was also much inspired by the level of persistence demonstrated in his entrepreneurial bio-CNG funding endeavour enroute to the third wealth ladder. It is very good to hear his personal voice with keen references to Joseph Conrad, Dreyfus & Dreyfus and many others."—**Ole Fryd, Associate Professor, Urban and Environmental Planning, University of Copenhagen, Denmark**

"My recommended read for anyone interested in how we develop as profession-als. The Professional Project Manager *is a must read and highly useful for anyone at any stage of their career. The book offers a balanced and insightful take on what it takes to become good at what we do. It will give you new reference points, stir your mental models and change your perspectives."*
—**Hope Segone, CEO, Mathaholo Group, South Africa**

"Linking project management to recent advances of humanity, this is an invaluable guide for professional project managers, and anyone, trying to understand the paradoxical character of the context and experiences that makes us better. Immensely useful inspiration both to those new to the subject and to the very experienced."—**Frans Bévort, PhD, Associate Professor, Copenhagen Business School, Denmark**

"I had the pleasure of reading the new project management book by Mr Laugesen. What sets the book apart is its focus not only on technical aspects but also on human, power and complex uncertain aspects of project manage-ment. It is a book that undoubtedly will enhance your project management skills. Laugesen's clear and concise writing style makes complex project man-agement concepts easy to understand and apply. I particularly appreciated the practical tips and real-world examples provided throughout the book. It is evident that the author through experiences gained from a lifetime in project management in both government and private organizations has a deep under-standing of the subject matter and a passion for helping others succeed in their project management journeys. The Professional Project Manager *provides*

professional life lessons for us all. I highly recommend it!"—**Koketso Molefi, Managing Director, Thaga Engineering, South Africa**

"The Professional Project Manager *is important and accessible in equal measure, with a balance between examples presented as stories and lessons learned and analytics set out with clarity and verve. With a starting point in project management,* The Professional Project Manager *spans a rich range of topics and is a highly readable yet deeply informed reflection on what becoming good at our profession requires."*—**Siyanda Mngadi, Geophysicist, South Africa**

"*Laugesen's approach is experience-based, projects stories and lessons learned, but he has done his legwork so they cumulate into a persuasive theoretical whole, a highly informative book."*—**Dr. Sarawut Srisakuna, President of the Academician and Research Promotion Association, Bangkok**

Why Experience Matters

Nobody is born a professional; it is something we only become over time and with experience. Some professional capacities we learn by ourselves. Some we must learn from others. This book is about the critical experiences and mental models that make us better project managers and better professionals.

I have, for four decades, joined professionals all over the world in different work settings and organizations to plan, implement, and evaluate specific projects and tasks. I have been a project manager and team leader for 225 projects and worked in 24 countries[1] and I hope I can give depth to the critical experiences and capacities we must acquire to sustain our career. The entry point is *project management*, as this is where I have gained my professional depth. This entry point is used as a platform to discuss what in general makes us become good professionals and makes us good at what we do.

A key issue for me has always been how to develop relevant frameworks or mental models that address the realities we operate in, the realities of technique, people, power, and the unforeseen. Our capacity to deal with these realities starts out in a rather shallow way, but during our career, we attain more complex and nuanced capacities. We get better each time we have been involved *deep and long* in a task to understand its context complexities and we get better when we get exposed to different experiences and contexts. We get better because we are constantly learning. Every new experience alters what we know and how we act. Getting reminded of our previous experiences makes us process new experiences better than we did last time. What this accumulation of experiences means for how good we are and can become as project managers, as professionals, is a central theme of the book.

The book is a guided tour that starts with an origin story. Our own professional origin story is a story each one of us must write. I present my origin story in Chapter 1. Then, in Chapter 2, I move on to the fundamentals of becoming a professional project manager, a true professional.

Chapter 3 provides paths and lessons learned for accumulation of professional reference points, while the focus of Chapter 4 is on paths to navigate our technical, people, power, and complex unforeseen professional contexts and agendas. Chapter 5 provides broader contexts that anchor us as professionals, anchors we must know if we want to act professional. Chapter 6 concludes the tour with a look at our future professional context, a context characterized by collective distributed networks and bottom-up processes between billions of professionals. When we read something that could become professional reference points for us, we always need to validate the source, and this is covered in the *final* chapter.

The Professional Project Manager is about the reference points, experiences, contexts, and anchors most critical to acquire to become good project managers, good professionals, and good at what we do. There are today more than three billion professionals and hundreds of millions of project managers, and the critical experiences may be different for everyone, but they might also be more similar than we think. This book tries to cover the similarities—reference points and experiences we can learn from and mental models that make us think and act better. The differences are for each of us to experience.

CHAPTER 1

Origin Story

It is almost impossible not to think of our own professional life and path in terms of exceptionalism and uniqueness. But, in fact, our professional story and path are tales of normality and generality. I became an urban professional from a rural start, but I have not seen my own transition story in any rural–urban transition context. I have just lived, worked, and moved. It was just me, looking for opportunities, moving around. I never felt poor; I did not move from a rural to an urban arrival city; I was not part of the urbanization trend or any global transition or stream in fact. But I was. Even when I read *Arrival City* by Dough Saunders,[1] the coin fell. This was not my story, but theirs. But it was also my story.

I was born and lived the first years of my life in Plougstrup, the city of plows, in the sandy parts of western Jutland in Denmark. Plougstrup consisted of three farmhouses, two on one side of the gravel road and one on the other. We stayed at the dense northern side of the city. You would pass the city without knowing you had been there. My parents had one of the small farm holdings, which was a result of the Danish land redistribution where large farms were carved up into smaller farms. The farms were, of course, not sustainable and we were among the many small farmers leaving for the city. The school in Plougstrup consisted of one classroom containing all grade 1 to 9 students and one teacher. My brother and I shared a 10 m^2 room. We did not know or realize that we were poor and that my parents were forced to move from our rural living far away to the city. We moved 50 km north to the suburban arrival city of Bryndum with around 1,000 citizens and real suburban houses. Bryndum was located 20 km outside the real, and for us huge, city of Esbjerg with 40,000 people, which we, as children, however, never saw as it was too far away. My father got a job in the construction industry and my mother cleaned richer people's houses. My brother and I got a 15 m^2

room to share, and I stayed there happily for 12 years during primary and high school.

At high school, I was the quiet student, pretty much trying to get along unnoticed. My sociology teacher, however, decided, for reasons unknown to me, to give me good written *and* oral grades whether I uttered a word or not. I, and most others, at the time did, of course, never speak to him or other teachers. This unexpected expression of confidence in my abilities did have an impact that I became rather good in his subject. He probably would have no recollection of this, but it did, I think, have an impact on my professional route, and I chose to go further north, to the city of Aalborg of 75,000 citizens, to study at the university, as the first ever in my family on both my father's and mother's side. I moved into my 20 m² student apartment with own kitchen, bathroom, and all. After initial detours into economics and sociology, I set my focus first on public administration and later strategic management. In the last two years of my studies, I further specialized in international aspects of organizations, was outstationed one year to Thailand, and finalized university with a thesis on the political and organizational aspects of Kampuchean refugees in Thailand.

After university, I applied the shotgun approach to job seeking, got a job at Copenhagen municipality, and moved east to the biggest city in Denmark, Copenhagen, with 600,000 citizens. Here, I moved into a rented apartment of 50 m² in the district of Nørrebro, the poorest and the most multicultural part of Copenhagen, regarded by all in rural Jylland as extremely dangerous. It took my grandmother 10 years before she dared to drive the 250 km to visit me. Most of my university friends moved to Copenhagen; some, mostly the least ambitious, returned after a few years to Jylland to be closer to friends and family, while the rest settled into big city life. After my first job in Copenhagen municipality, I continued to become a consultant at the national association for municipalities, also located in Copenhagen. After working for seven years with implementation of organizational development projects in the public administration in Denmark, I thought my professional route was paved.

But some unforeseen events, such as a divorce, take us in unexpected directions and I suddenly found myself working as a production manager at my brother's clothing company in Bangkok. This unanticipated change meant that I returned to my interest in going international. As production of children's clothes was not exactly my field of interest or competence, I started to look for international options in my own professional field. This initially proved to be difficult: The international field was a rather closed-circuit field of people with long international CVs, and I had to go through a domestic position in an engineering consultancy company based in Copenhagen for a year, before getting myself squeezed into the international division of that company. I have since then only worked outside my country of birth, which involved in design, implementation, and evaluation of projects all over the world—first on numerous short-term assignments; then as a project manager on two 4-year ministerial capacity development projects, one in Borneo and another in Bangkok; then as a diplomat at the Danish Embassy in South Africa; and finally, the last decade, as an entrepreneur in South Africa. Constant circling of the globe to undertake assignments during the last decades took me more permanently to Kota Kinabalu with 200,000 citizens, Bangkok with 10 million people, and finally to Johannesburg in Gauteng Province with more than 15 million people.

Each turn and change in our professional life has its own different and specific reasons. If I consider each turn, I always find that what seemed like a rational personal choice, an obvious turn, or even a planned career move becomes less rational. We mostly try to explain our choices at the personal level and, when at this level, we either postrationalize or get confused as the factors are many, coincidental, and interlinked. It can be valuable to understand our turns and moves from the big picture perspective. And, here, a few things are clear. I moved from a tiny rural setting to bigger and bigger cities. My personal living space together with my financial abilities became better and better. And, through my own rural–urban transition, I became both a professional and an urban globalist.

Still, it was first by reading something by someone who had dedicated serious effort and energy to study and understand a phenomenon from the view of many, over a historical and geographical span, that I really got a grip of this rural–urban professionalizing context. When I read Dough Saunders' *Arrival City*, my understanding and knowledge of the rural–urban transition, and the middle-class professionalizing it brings along, jumped several levels up in one go. Saunders' book hit a personal nerve in my own rural–urban transition and got me thinking of the connections between individual experience, knowledge, and big picture contexts. The rural–urban transition has and will continue to deeply influence our professional context. This massive rural–urban movement will affect directly more than three billion people in this century, three billion people! We must be clear and fully aware of its causes and consequences. That is why we read—how else would we know?

We will end this century as a wholly urban species. It will be the last human movement of this size, and the changes it makes to family life, from large agrarian families to small urban ones, will put an end to population growth. When almost the entire world is urban, this will mark an end point. Once we urbanize, we almost never return. The first time we made such a dramatic migration, the direct effect was a complete reinvention of human thought, governance, technology, professions, and welfare. Mass urbanization produced the French Revolution, the Industrial Revolution, and, with them, the enormous social and political changes of the previous two centuries. We are, today, in the final great human migration: 300 million Chinese farmers floating between village and city, vast shifts under way in India, and huge numbers of Africans and Southeast Asians joining the city-bound journey. By 2050, more than 70 percent of the world will live in cities.

The rural–urban migration is in any measurable sense an improvement. It is a force of lasting progress, an end to poverty, a more sustainable economy, and a less brutal existence compared to the village. There is and has never been any romance in village life. Rural living is the largest single killer of humans today and the greatest source of malnutrition, infant mortality, and reduced lifespans. Three-quarters of the world's billion people living in hunger are farmers. Mortal poverty is a rural phenomenon. Urban incomes everywhere are higher, often by large multiples compared to rural income, and access to education, health, water, and sanitation as well as communications and culture is always better in the city. The dramatic recent declines in the number of very poor people in the world, with hundreds of millions of people having left poverty just in the last decade, were caused entirely by urbanization through arrival cities.

These arrival cities are known around the world by many names: slums, favelas, shantytowns, kampongs, and informal settlements. To an outsider, arrival cities are fetid slums—shambles of thrown-together houses, dirt laneways lined with phone shops, butchers, street-side eateries, dirt, plastic, and smells everywhere. Having been raised and having studied in Denmark, big city slum is not something I grew up having experience with. The first time I saw slum was on my first travel around the world as a 21-year-old. In Bangkok, Manila, India, and Pakistan, I saw slum by walking around and watching people in their slum. I was thinking, as most are, this is bad and depressing and some-body should do something about it. This is poverty at its worst. And I could not have been more wrong. The second time I experienced slum was in Bangkok as a 26-year-old studying at Chulalongkorn University. Some of the staff invited me to their homes, which rather shockingly for me were slum dwellings on the outskirts of Bangkok. I saw them come out of the slums, clean, sharply dressed, and ready for work and wondered how they did this. But I had been to their homes and, however small and cramped, they were always organized, clean, and orderly. I noticed, wondered, and went back home to finish my studies. Later, through my assignments all over the world, my experience with slum and people liv-ing in slums increased—local counterparts and staff; good, hardworking colleagues and professionals. But, still, I did not really know where they came from, why they were staying in slums, and what their common story was. I knew now not to feel bad as I could see that they lived a normal life, with all the normal worries of people, friends, work, family, lovers, and children, but I did not really know the context. I read 3,000 persons arrive every day in Johannesburg, where I now stay, and still ignorantly wondered how this is possible; where do they arrive; where do they stay; and how do so many people, without anything, survive this arrival to the big city. And how in the world did the city plan for and cope with this massive daily influx.

By reading Sanders' *Arrival City*, I realized that things are not always what they seem. I got a hold of what the real functions of these slums, or arrival cities, are. The arrival cities exist to bring villagers and entire villages into the urban sphere, into the center of social and economic life, into education and sustainable prosperity, and into the professional middle class. The main functions of arrival cities are arrival and transition. The arrival city can be distinguished from other urban neighborhoods by the constant linkages it makes, from every street and every house, in two directions. It is linked intensively to its originating villages, constantly sending people, money, and knowledge back and forth, making possible the next wave of immigration from the village, facilitating within the village the care of older generations and the education of the younger ones, and financing the improvement of the village. And it is linked to the established city and its business relationships, social networks, and transactions which are all footholds intended to give the new village arrivals a purchase, however fragile, on the edge of the larger city, and to give them a place to push themselves, and their children, further into the center, into acceptability and connectedness.

Arrival cities are the sites where the transition from poverty occurs. In these places are people who have been born in villages, who have their minds and ambitions fixed on the symbolic center of the city, and who are engaged in a struggle of monumental scope to find a basic and lasting berth in the city for themselves and their children. Arrival cities are often seen as static appendages, cancerous growths on an otherwise healthy city. This is to completely ignore the arrival city's great success: An arrival city is the key mechanism in abolishing the horrors of rural poverty, ending inequality, and creating a new professional middle class. Everyone who lives here has arrived from a rural village. Everyone who remains here beyond a few months has decided to stay for the long haul, despite the filth, crowding, and difficulty of life, and even though the children are often, at first, left behind with family members back in the village, they have decided that this is a better life. Almost all send money, often almost all of their earnings, back to support the village and put some into savings for their children's education in the city. All are engaged in a daily calculation that involves the unbearable burden of rural deprivation and the impossible expense of full-fledged urban life. Nowhere in the world do we find rural families packing up en masse and moving at once to the city. It does not happen that way. The world's population shifts cityward in a back-and-forth oscillation of single individuals and clusters of villagers, pushed and pulled by tides of agriculture, economy, and climate. The main mechanism is chain migration, which moves groups of related individuals or households from one place to another via social arrangements in which people at the destination provide aid, information, and encouragement to new migrants. Chain migration is the process by which seasonal migrants are pulled into the city and turned into urbanites. By turning from circular migrants into fixed arrival-citizens who aid the future migration of others, they establish a more secure, village-related urban base. This is the pattern of arrival cities everywhere: Nations do not migrate, but regions and villages do. Once the links have been established between the peripheral arrival city and the village community of origin, migration tends to be direct to that specific arrival city. When arrival cities are understood in the light of oscillating chain migrations, it is easy to see their importance for both urban and rural development. They are not slums housing the outcasts and failures of the urban society, nor are they temporary encampments for transient labor. They are the key mechanism for rural development and the economic growth of cities.

The ones who stay on experience that the informal, entrepreneurial self-employed economy of the arrival city, even though more chaotic, is providing better livelihoods than their old village economy. They are not ignorant and desperate peasants blindly seeking opportunity; they are well informed, making a calculated move from a rural to an urban life. We see repeated today around the globe the out-of-poverty arrival city mechanism we saw effectively doing the job at the end of the 18th century in the New World. And what arrival cities produce are among the most inventive and resilient population groups in the world. Contrary to their popular image as the losers in a capitalist society, the individuals and families who make it into the slums are the winners of the rural–urban lottery, the best of the best from the villages, the most successful of a highly ambitious group. The migrants from the villages come with very high expectations, often higher than those of the native-born city dwellers. They always have the choice to move out and go back to the village, and some of them do. Those who stay are the toughest and smartest and they can take a lot of change. Many arrival city residents, often after only a decade, remarkably end up having better economic and social standing than many native-born residents of the city. In other words, the unimpeded arrival city is a more effective form of development than any other known economic, social, or population-control development policy. Many economists and some governments have realized that rural–urban migration, far from being a problem for poor countries, is the key to their economic futures. The World Bank has concluded that the most effective route to poverty reduction and economic growth is to encourage the highest possible urban population density and the growth of as large cities as possible through rural–urban migration.

The transformation to the real city is the gauge of the arrival city: People flow through it and transform into full-fledged contributors to the life of the city. They, in general, make the journey from a rural shack to the center of middle-class urban life within one or two generations. This is the core function of the arrival city; it is the sole objective for all those hundreds of millions of journeys from village to city. Rural migrants consider this transformation the norm. In fact, they expect it. The move from village to city is always a calculated effort to raise a family's living standard, income, and quality of life, using the arrival city as its main instrument. Arrival city poverty, despite its crowding and frequent humiliations, is an improvement on rural poverty, and no arrival city resident considers poverty anything but a temporary necessity. The arrival city is only the first step in a journey planned carefully by the migrant. Nobody invests their entire life, and a generation's income and peace, simply to move from one form of poverty to another. The residents of arrival cities do not consider themselves the poor but rather successful urbanites who happen to be passing through a period of hardship, perhaps for a generation.

A successful arrival city sends out successful middle-class migrants to wealthier neighborhoods at rates similar to their intake of poor villagers. People move through its neighborhoods. This through-flow means that the arrival cities themselves often stay poor, but this is a result of the arrival city's success as it is constantly sending its educated second generation into more prosperous neighborhoods and taking in waves of new villagers, in a constantly reiterated cycle of arrival, upward mobility, and exodus. This paradox has created a sense among outsiders that arrival cities are poorer or more desperate than they really are, which leads to a misunderstanding of the forms of government investment they need. Rather than getting the tools of land ownership, education, business creation, and connection to the wider economy, they are too often treated as destitute places that need nonsolutions such as social workers, public-housing blocks, or urban-planned redevelopments. What arrival city residents most need is the opportunity to start a business and be educated;

thereafter an arrival city takes care of itself, its residents know what to do, they have been doing it for years, and they and their children will become part of the city, and a whole new professional middle class will develop.

The arrival city mechanism made the professional middle class in 2018 the biggest group in the world: 3.8 billion professional middle classers to be precise.[2] Not only is the global professional middle class now a majority, but it is also the most rapidly growing group expected to reach 5.3 billion by 2030. Two billion are Asians and that number is set to increase to 3.5 billion by 2030. This means that there will be 10 times more professional middle classers in Asia than in North America and five times more than Europe—truly stunning numbers. Latin America's 180 million and Africa's 170 million professional middle classers will have doubled by 2030, while Europe's 500 million middle classers will have stabilized by 2030. We move toward a world where four out of five people are professional middle classers, already the case in some countries in Northern Europe. In the countries I have worked, the professional middle-class percentage has given me a good mental model of where I am in relation to so many factors. In South Africa, 15 percent are professionals, while Mozambique only has 5 percent, very few professionals to mingle with. Denmark's 80 percent means that almost everyone you meet is a middle classer with a professional education and background.

The growth of the professional middle class is the driver of a host of welcome changes.[3] The world's recent progress in reducing the number of people living in extreme poverty is a consequence of the exploding middle class. The typical professional middle classers are born rural or, in an arrival city, moved to the big city and tend to be a competitive hardworking bunch. Professional middle classers set goals and strive to achieve them. They work hard, plan ahead, and expect to save to attain their goals. They adapt to stay relevant and undertake lifelong learning to secure adaptability to the changing market demands. They raise their children to value work and education because they know their children will be dependent upon work, not capital, land, or inheritance, for their income. They convey to their children the principle that if you work hard within the system and follow the rules, you will get ahead. They pass down the patience necessary for children to pursue an education, career, or entrepreneurial activity. They drive demand in the global economy.

Their growth creates a spiral of increased professional specialization that creates global innovation and wealth. They demand and support good governance and democracy and create social stability. They are vocal, powerful, and dominate voting patterns when they are more than a third of the population. They put pressure on governments to perform better (a few professional middle classers are directly linked to poor bureaucratic quality, instability, lack of democratic accountability, and corruption). They create higher levels of trust resulting in less time and resources spent on verification and policing. (It was in South Africa, with its still small middle class, that I had to hire a lawyer for the first time in my life. Lawyers are everywhere here; the biggest and most extravagant buildings in the richest parts of Johannesburg belong to law firms; the skyline is a who's who of global and local law firms. Any transaction or disagreement has a good chance of requiring a lawyer to mediate. Companies, government, staff, and garden workers take you to court on the slightest opportunity. Trust is a rarer commodity in South Africa.)

Education, occupation, lifestyle, ethic and financial resources—I cannot escape being a professional middle classer. I have come to not only see but also appreciate my middle-class traits. Postponements of needs and delayed gratification, that's me. I had my first professional salary at 29 and my first car at 32 (an old Daihatsu Charade). I am grounded in the ethic of making sacrifices in the short term to pave way for greater success in the long term. Being able to delay gratification is for me a marker of professional character. I am willing to accept smaller benefits in the short term to have professional partners with whom to cooperate and sustain myself in the long run. I am never a cheater or thief. I have started to always announce loudly and clearly that I am a global professional middle classer. That is my home. I told one of my professional friends here in South Africa that I was a middle classer, and he just looked at me. With the label comes not only my ethical and moral anchoring, but also the more profane financial ability anchoring. I have recently entered and become a financial global one percenter, as dollar millionaires today account for more than 1 percent of the global population for the first time in history; 56.1 million professionals have assets worth more than a million dollars, which is a lot of rich professionals. However, South Africa only has 36,500 dollar millionaires, or 0.1 percent, so here I am a part of a much smaller group, that's why his stare. If I had stayed in Denmark, I would have been a 5.3 percenter.

The world will, in the coming few decades, see a couple of billion new professional middle classers and most of these newcomers will come directly from rural villages through the arrival city mechanism. They will be a huge bunch of determined and hardworking new rural-born middle-class professionals. And because of this—their numbers, their rural upbringing, and their determination and mentality—they will change everything. Nobody today can image the magnitude of the changes these billions of determined new rural to urban professionals will bring along in the coming decades. I was and am one of them.

That was my origin story framed: where I come from, why did I end up with the profession and values I have, what paths I took, what big picture transitions I was and am part of. When we read something professionally, we need to validate the source, and an origin story is a kind of validation story.

My origin story is also a story that frames the themes for becoming a professional project manager; it is a story that sets the story line for the rest of the book: the need to continuously accumulate experiences and reference points to know what we talk about and to know what we do not know; the need to mix personal experiences with reference points we get from others; to understand contexts; the need to know our numbers and facts; to recognize patterns and realize that things are not always what they seem; and to know that frequency and repetition increase memory strength and that memorable mental models are valuable. I hope you will not forget arrival cities and what it means. I repeated the word 44 times. The need to know the broader contexts that anchors us. And the need to know what is ahead of us. The arrival of billions of new motivated rural-anchored professionals and project managers is one of them.

What gives us our professional capacity is a mix of four factors: our personal origin story, accumulation of reference points, our ability to recognize different professional contexts, and the broader context that anchors us. It is when we understand and blend these four factors that we become good professional project managers—good professionals. I will get to that but first to the fundamentals.

CHAPTER 2

Fundamentals

The fundamentals to become good at what we do are *accumulation* of professional reference points and *spreading activation* to utilize these reference points. Accumulation of professional reference points and experiences, and in particular the accumulation of technical, people, power, and complex unforeseen professional experiences, is the starting point for becoming a professional project manager. The brain's spreading activation system is the mechanism that handles this accumulation of professional reference points and makes us think and act professionally. It is from these fundamental platforms we go to work and become good project managers and good professionals.

The Five Levels

I, like all professionals, have tried to become better and better at what I do and to move upward from the first professional capacity level obtained at the university. This upward movement, in my experience, is intrinsically linked to an acceptance of the fact that there *are* different levels of professional capacity and that these capacity levels play out on different playing fields. This acceptance, how obvious it might seem, requires modesty and maturity because it forces us to accept that sometimes we, in relation to specific issues and understandings, may only be at level 1 or 2. We must accept, throughout our professional life, that sometimes for some things we are a bit dumb and inexperienced and that we cannot be a qualified minister at 22, an efficient CEO of a large international company at 35, or have valuable opinions of how complex real-life systems work at 28. It does not work that way not because we are not clever but because we have not seen enough different contexts and not accumulated enough different reference points.

Six persons were videotaped independently while they were undertaking resuscitation of patients through heart massage and artificial respiration. Five of the six were inexperienced students currently being trained in life recovery. The sixth was a professional with solid experience in resuscitation. These videos were then shown to three different groups: professionals with practical experience in resuscitation, teachers in resuscitation, and students in the discipline. Each spectator was asked: Which of the six persons on the videos would you choose to resuscitate you if you had an accident? The experienced professionals chose in 90 percent the experienced professional. The students only got it correct in 50 percent of the cases, while, surprisingly, the teachers only got it right in 30 percent of the cases. What kind of rationality did make the teachers perform so poorly and what were the reasons for the experienced professionals to choose correctly?[1]

Dreyfus and Dreyfus's five levels of professional capacity[2] remind us that we always start out a bit weak and from there move toward deeper and deeper professional understandings of achievements, contexts, balances, paradoxes, and dilemmas—professional understandings we are not born with but acquire—accumulated experiences and reference points being the key. The more often we have seen or met a specific issue, context, or problem, the better and faster we understand it and can react to it. As the understanding and acknowledgment of these levels of professional capacity are so important, let me start by giving some detail to the content of our five professional capacity levels.

At the *first level*, we meet a problem or a situation for the first time. By instruction and training, we learn to recognize different objective facts and characteristics of the situation, and rules for action are taught. Facts, characteristics, and rules are defined so clearly that they can be recognized without being related to the specific, concrete situation they operate within. They can be generalized for all similar situations. On this level, we value and are valued upon how well we follow the rules we have learned. The first rules are necessary to accumulate our own first professional experiences, but these rules slowly become a hindrance in the professional learning process.

We advance from the first to the *second level* by gaining experience from real life, contrary to the theoretical and protected situations at the first level. Through these experiences, we start to recognize relevant elements in relevant situations. The recognition happens because we see similarities to earlier examples of similar situations. The recognition is concrete and dependent of context. Rules for action are on this level, therefore, both context dependent and independent.

On the ***third level***, we are taught, of others and ourselves, to apply a hierarchical, prioritizing procedure for decision making. By choosing a goal and a plan, organizing the information of the specific situation, and only dealing with the important and relevant factors, we can both simplify and improve our results and achievements. Goals, plans, and prioritizing make us deal with a more limited set of important factors instead of having to deal with the combined and total knowledge of a given situation. Competent doers on this level display a quicker interpretative mode of thinking and action, quite dissimilar to the slow analytical mode of thinking that characterizes rational problem solving at the first levels. We are beginning to get better adapted to the specific context at this level. To choose a plan, however, is not simple and without problems. It takes time and on this level it is still done consciously and carefully. The choice of plan has extensive consequences for actions and results. The blurred fix points for the choice of plan, combined with the necessity to have a plan, result in a new key issue: involvement. At the first levels, we only experienced limited responsibility for the results of our actions. We used trained elements and prescribed rules to undertake actions. A bad result would, if not made by a direct mistake, appear to be the result of insufficient rules. On this level, this does not hold. Here we are involved in the actions with our own person. After having struggled with the problem of choice of plan, we feel responsible for the consequences of the choice. *Interpretation and judgment* are therefore included in the actions on this level. These two elements are at the core of true professional capacity and expertise and become even more crucial at the last two capacity levels.

So far, we have, if not only abiding rules and prescriptions, still only made choices of goals, decisions, and actions after careful reflections of different alternatives. Contrary to this, the decision-making process on the ***fourth level*** is more fluid and less phased in time. We are, on this level, deeply involved in our actions and have developed a *perspective* on the basis of earlier situations and experiences. This perspective makes certain aspects in a situation stand out more clearly while others are more nondistinctive and less important. New situations and experiences will change the aspects that stand out, change the plans and expectations and thereby actions. A rational choice of aims and plans, or a conscious assessment of problems and solutions, is not undertaken. The choice, assessment, and judgment are plainly made, but made based on our earlier experience with similar situations. We understand and organize our tasks more fluidly but still occasionally think analytically on what should happen. Elements and plans that stand out as important and relevant are assessed and combined analytically with the help of rules to get the most appropriate decisions. The deep experience-based involvement is interchanged with analytical decision making.

Slowly we might reach a point where it is not only situations that are recognized fluidly but also the relevant decisions, strategies, and actions that are judged and done synchronously, coherently, and comprehensively. The professional on this *fifth level* will in a normal and well-known situation not virtuously solve tasks or make decisions but just do what normally works. Neither will the professional expert never think rational nor always get it right. The unforeseen and unexpected will always happen. Wicked contexts or ambiguity is something that even the professional expert only sometimes can counterbalance.[3] The professional on this level acts based on mature, holistic experience-based understandings seemingly without any conscious deliberations and does not see problems as one thing and solutions as something else. Often the professional do not even make a plan. When asked to put the reasons for acting into principles or rules of thumb, these explanations mostly look like after-the-fact rationalizations, not obviously linked to or even incongruent with the actual actions and results achieved.

The five levels as a mental model. I think everyone with decades of professional experience can recognize themselves in these descriptions of the different levels of capacity. When I was in my 30s, I was obsessed with how-to-do checklists. In my 40s, I submersed myself in plans, logical framework analyses, and analytical stuff. In my 50s, things became more fluid, but I am still drawn to making complicated diagrams, boxes, and checklists, which, I know from experience, no experienced professional will ever look at.

The five levels of professional capacity give us a mental model with important insights. They are why it is so important not to use checklists blindfolded; why some people do better than others; why experience and teams with different types of contextual experience are so important; and why some systems and projects are designed to not work—because they are designed by people with a level-one professional experience.

The five-level mental model also reminds us that putting in the hours is not enough. It is often said that it takes 10,000 hours of practice to become an expert or a master performer in any given field. The most accomplished violin students have put in 10,000 hours by the time they turn 20. Unfortunately, professionalism in complex settings does not really link to the 10,000-hour rule. The rule points in the right direction—we must put in the hours to get experience, but it skips the steps of Dreyfus and Dreyfus' capacity levels where it is not just the hours put in but the accumulation of in-depth reference points and contextual variance over the long haul that matters. It might work for a violinist or football player, but professionals cannot just put in the technical hours and then we are there as professionals. From level three, an important change in our professional capacity happens because the most important basis for action is no longer analytical rule thinking but context and accumulated experience. Action based on logic is superseded by experience-based action. The five-level model makes us remember that analytical rationality does not show us the full spectrum of professional capacities. When the first two levels are treated as all there is, as the only mode for professional capacity, or as being sufficient levels of capacity to reach, analytic rule-based rationality comes in the way of good results and real professional achievements. But it is also important to recognize that the first levels provide basic, professional approaches we must know as we cannot go to levels three, four, or five without having passed levels one and two.

The Four Contexts

Dreyfus and Dreyfus showed that for increased professional capacity context is everything. But what is this context thing that is so important. Ask any experienced professional, a project manager, a headmaster, a chief surgeon, an engineer, a CEO, a government manager, or an economist, what it takes to be good, effective, and resourceful in his or her field. The answer is always the same: Of course, I need to be technically good or even the best but that alone is far from enough to make me a good professional who creates real results and has an impact in the area I work in. I need to be able to control, manage, and be concerned about a huge number of equally important issues. I need to motivate, sell the things I want to achieve to people inside and outside my organization, control power games, and react when situations change, and I need luck.

At the start of our career, on the first two capacity levels, we pretty much can concentrate our efforts on getting the technical aspects of our profession right and becoming technically better and better at what we do. However, on the next capacity levels, where context becomes equally important to create results and impact, we need to establish, develop, and utilize contextual skills, on top of the continued improvement of our technical skills. Experienced professionals operate in interconnected, multilayered, and fast-changing surroundings, and we must have the ability to grasp these contextual features. To improve, we must have a useful mental model of the fundamental contexts wherein our professional capacities exist.

I have found it useful to understand our professional context in relation to four distinctive perspectives: *Technical, People, Power, and Unforeseen complexity (TPPU)*. Each of these four perspectives gives a distinct insight into and understanding of how our professional context operates and *provide a mental model* of the types of contextual capacities we need to acquire to perform professionally.

Why these four perspectives? First, because they make sense. They make sense for me when I try to understand what is going on around me and how this influences my attempts to influence direction, processes, aims, and goals. The importance of this cognitive resonance should not be underestimated. Mental models are theoretical generalizations, but they are also and must be useful tools. It is not sufficient to say that to act professionally I must be concerned about a huge number of equally important contextual issues. I need a professional contextual mental model that will guide my thinking and actions.

But also they are the outcome of the last more than hundred years of studies and attempts to understand professional context, structures, behavior, decision making, actions, results, and impacts. The understanding of our professional context as a technical-rational machine was developed and applied from the 1900s onward, the people-oriented perspective from the 1950s, the political power perspective from the 1970s, and the complexity perspective from the 1990s onward. The fact that these four professional context perspectives received different attention during the past century does not mean that they were not there before they were studied and described. They have always been there. Technical rationality, people, power, and complex unforeseen unpredictability are something professionals always have had to deal with. The complex adaptive system perspective, though, has recently become more important as both the rapid global population growth and the second globalization have made everything more interlinked, fast-paced, and unpredictable than ever before. Let me give details to the content of these four different contexts for our professional capacity. Furthermore, let me put them into their own historical emergence context.

Context 1: *The rational machine. We are surrounded by technical rationality.* The understanding of our professional context as a rational machine can be traced all the way back to Newtonian physics, where our context is presented as stable, predictable, and having clearly discernible causes and effects. Later, Weber saw bureaucracy as a form that could achieve the highest degree of societal rationality with rational, rule-oriented and impersonal features. The scientific management school by Taylor, Fayol, and Mintzberg added focus on optimizing the professional work processes and organizational structures, and the economists added the idea of the rational economic man. Understanding of our professional context as a rational machine remains central today as bureaucracy and rational machine organization have proven to be a very economical and efficient way to solve clearly defined tasks. The application of the machine model can lead to predictable, reliable, and fast outcomes and in public bureaucratic systems to transparency and fairness. Professional capacities in this perspective are linked to efficiency, calculations, predictability, planning, clear and transparent objectives, outputs, responsibilities, deadlines, and budgets. People and organizations in this context are portrayed as rational and well-functioning machines with clear and straightforward purposes. No conflicting needs, hidden agendas, or chaos here. The inertia and inflexibility of the machine organization, however, became a theoretical and practical problem in the second half of the past century, external in relation to a lack of ability to adapt to changes, internal by attempting to deny important features of our human nature. We do not function well in cages, and new understandings of our professional context developed in the last part of the past century.

Context 2: The human system. We are surrounded by people. We always operate in a context of other people. In the fields of sociology, psychology, and anthropology evolved from the 1950s onward a new perspective to our professional context emphasizing the complexity of humans, human processes, and interactions. Professional capacities are, in this second context perspective, linked to competences, commitments, wishes, longings, participation, involvement, and motivation in and around the work–life context. This perspective led to adjustments of the machine perspective and led to organizations that became even more efficient and innovative by adding a focus on competence, motivation, and involvement. Our professional context is in this perspective primarily seen as harmonic with motivated, involved professionals with no conflicts of interest, power struggles, or other unpleasantries. This became the platform for the perspective that came next.

Context 3: The political power system. We are surrounded by power struggles. In the machine and people perspectives, professionals undertake specific well-defined tasks, and it is pretended that it is possible to avoid the role or use of politics, power, and conflicts. From the late 1960s, an understanding evolved that departed from these perspectives and instead focused on our professional context as a political system. The academic fields of political science, sociology, philosophy, social constructivism, and symbolism (my initial fields of study) used the political perspective to understand our professional context as centers for power, interests, influence, coalitions, conflict, and struggle for resources. Professionals here deal with conflicting power centers, with the effective formulation and use of political power, with front- or backstage activities to reach outputs and aim, and with the use of symbols and symbolic actions to gain support, legitimacy, and acceptance. Power and influence are in many respects backstage and taboo and that might explain why the revival period became relatively short and why the view had few followers or practical impacts, even though issues like conflict management became more prominent. Still, the political power perspective adds important insights into real aspects of our professional context.

Context 4: The complex emergent system. We are surrounded by complexity, unpredictability, and emergence. The people and political perspectives to our professional context attempt to part with or modify the logic of the machine perspective, but still share with it the idea of controlled contexts, where professionals are placed in the role of controllers. By using our intellect, charm, and power, we make things happen and control structures, behaviors, power, and outcomes. Over the past few decades, new perspectives that stress very different contextual aspects have emerged. Uncontrollable processes, complexities, uncertainties, coincidences, chaos, and powers external to our knowledge are here in focus and we are left with a humbler and more reduced role in relation to the chains of occurrences and contexts we are part of. These new perspectives build on the sciences of chaos, complex adaptive systems, and nonlinear dynamics and focus on complexity, emergence, and adaptation. They all provide new ways of thinking about causality in our professional context. Contexts are here complex and chaotic and contain complex processes of involvement of a vast number of actors pulling in different directions. There is, here, no overriding system or method but primarily many small steps, processes, and interactions making up the context. Transformation and development happen through self-organizing processes, not through big plans or top-down strategic planning. This perspective fills in valuable gaps in the understanding of our professional context, including why we continue to see so many failures and outcomes not planned for. The perspective has had little impact on how we talk about professional capacities and contexts, but this does not mean it has had little impact. In the real world, the perspective has just continued to implement itself.

The Spreading Activation Mechanism

Accumulation of professional *experiences* and an understanding of the four *contexts* that anchor these professional experiences are two fundamentals for becoming a good project manager, a true professional. Our ability to *recollect* these reference points, experiences, and contexts leads us to the third fundamental, the understanding of how the memory of professional reference points works through a spreading activation mechanism.

Our brain with all its stored semantic, episodic, nondeclarative memories, metamemory, mental models, firing neurons, and spreading activation is remarkable. The computational power of millions and millions of dense connections between neurons in the brain enables us to recognize our friends, read a book, solve problems, think about our professional work, and make strategic plans. Spreading activation is how the brain iterates through a network of associated reference points, experiences, and ideas to retrieve specific information. Spreading activation is the search for associative semantic, episodic, or nondeclarative memory networks. All this takes place through the automatic process of neuronal firing through electrical impulses and neurotransmitters.

Spreading activation

To understand how this works, and how we can utilize and moderate storage and recollection of professional reference points through the spreading activation mechanism, is easier said than done. Our mind is a bit of mystery to us, and to understand our brain, our memories, and the spreading activation mechanism is quite a thing. For that, there is no way around reading. I read Mukherjee,[4] Pinker,[5] and Minda[6] and slowly got somewhere.

It all begins with our senses, our eyes and ears, perception, and sensory activation. Our *short-term working memory*, moderated by attention and inhibition, closely connects our short-term memory to perception of reference points and experiences. Our working memory is an intermediary between the world out there, what we see, experience, read, and hear, and the world in here, our world of *long-term memories*. Without long-term memory of our professional reference points and experiences, without being able to recollect and retrieve what we have experienced and learned, we would be amateurs, lost. Our long-term memory system is what allows us to learn things and to generalize and act professionally from past experiences and learnings. We tend to regard memory as a mental process analogous to a computer hard drive. We learn something and then we file that reference point or experience away in memory where it can be retrieved later as needed. It would be nice if professionalism was a thing, a fact some specific information or knowledge that we can recall and pronounce. But it is not. It is a mixed bag of many accumulated professional experiences, of many different technical, people, power, and complex adaptive learnings. It is many different professional memories and reference points blended somewhere in there in our brain.

We have episodic memories that are organized around personal experiences that occurred in the past, we have semantic memories that are factual in nature, and then we have memories that come to us more unconsciously. Our *episodic* memory records specific experiences, things that happened to us, any kind of thing, important or mundane, our last dinner, a colleague who said something polite, or the first day on a new job. These are episodes, personal experiences that happened to us in the past. Our episodic memory makes us individual professionals as it allows us to recall something that happened to us as an individual in the past, and it stores our conscious experience of who we are and what we have done. Our *semantic* memory is our memory system for facts and knowledge. These can be facts we know for certain, the name of places or colors, or it can be more complex mental models, such as globalization, demographic transition, and business cycles, which we develop into things we think we know as facts. Semantic memories have meaning, and they have labels and names. These fact-based semantic memories are organized conceptually. Our third type of memory is our *nondeclarative memories*. These span from how to grip a coffee mug to making advanced experience-based professional decisions. We know that we know them, but we cannot inspect them. We cannot really describe their content using language. We can try but fundamentally we cannot articulate or explain how these nondeclarative memories work. Their retrieval and use are automatic and outside of consciousness. Moreover, these memories are plentiful and important. We are constantly using and updating these nondeclarative professional memories without realizing it. Professional actions based on these automatic memories take a long time to acquire. But once we have learned them, they become effortless to undertake. Without the need to filter these memories through consciousness, without the need for attention and recall, these nondeclarative memories are fast and efficient. And then there is our *metamemory*, an awareness of what we know and what we do not know. When we experience something that we do not think we have experienced before, we use our metamemory to decide if we recognize the new experience or not. We use our metamemory to recognize the limits of our previous experiences and knowledge.

All our professional reference points, experiences, and knowledge, whether episodic, semantic, or nondeclarative, are stored in a *spreading activation system* as connections between clusters of neurons and distributed across different areas of our brain as states of activation. Within the spreading activation system, our reference points are organized in a *hierarchical similarity system*. If two professional reference points or experiences are similar to each other, they will be stored in a way that makes them seem close, and the more closely related two professional experiences or reference points are, the more quickly the activation spreads and the quicker we think and act. Furthermore, within the spreading activation system, the stored reference points will have different *strengths*. If reference points or experiences are frequent or often remembered, they will be encoded strongly and can be recollected more easily.

When we get better at what we do, we get better at recognizing the similarity between reference points and experiences that we received or experienced in the past and what is happening now. The recognition does not have to be overt and explicit, all that matters is that our brain is able to treat the correspondence between the current pattern of activation and the previous pattern of activation as being similar. The effect is automatic and unavoidable as we cannot ignore the cascade of neural activation that occurs when a current situation brings to mind previous, similar reference points or experiences. Based on this neural pattern recognition, we take decisions, solve problems, and make professional judgments.

When we accumulate professional reference points, our automatic spreading activation system has more to work with and takes a better hold. When I perform good and fast, I can sense the spreading activation system working in overdrive, I can almost feel the neurons fire, and I have a clear feeling that the spreading activation system helps me think quicker, act better, and do better in professional discussions and decisions. Spreading activation makes me confident.

For professionals, a unique professional reference point is where it all starts, it is *the* critical unit for neural firing, for our professional capacity, and accumulation of these unique professional reference points is the only way to move up the professional capacity ladder. Our memory and spreading activation system are not fuzzy about what constitutes a professional reference point. It can be our own experiences, each with unique contexts experienced by ourselves, it can be reference points we receive from others, other professional's experiences, stories, and knowledge, and it can be reference points from books, studies, and big data analysis. Each reference point and experience are added to our memory and used in the spreading activation mechanism. Each reference point is stored, each new reference point is added to the already stored reference points, and each reference point is compared to other similar reference points, and with time this comparison becomes exponential as more and more previous reference points are compared to the present professional reference point being experienced. Fortunately, exponentiality and complexity are reduced by comparison in similarity groups of similar reference points.

We store and retrieve reference points and experiences, but we think with concepts and mental models. Everything we experience, everything we have episodic, semantic, and nondeclarative memories of, we organize into *categories, concepts, and mental models*. A mental model condenses many experiences into one abstract representation. This means that although a group of professional reference points and experiences may be different and many in number, we may behave toward them in the same way. This is cognitive efficiency. The more familiar, the more efficiently our brain can understand it by conceptual combination and mental model referencing. Concepts and mental models provide structure to our professional mental world. These mental models are powered by regularities and pattern recognition, and a good part of becoming a professional is to learn about the regularities that exist in the external world, in our professional contexts. Using mental models to recognize patterns and regularities is what we, with experience, get better and better at.

There are several ways in which we can deliberately use the knowledge of how our brain, memories, and spreading activation work to improve our professional capacities. *We can actively strengthen the executive functions of our working memory,* especially the functions of attention and inhibition. These executive functions are how we control our thoughts and behavior and how we ignore something. This is important as we need to be able to ignore irrelevant or unnecessary thoughts or emotions, so that we devote more attention to relevant ones. Attention and inhibition are what we need for higher-order professional thinking and reasoning and for social interaction as we often need to inhibit our first reactions and respond in a more appropriate way. Inhibition is critical for getting things done. We need to inhibit our desire to check our phone every two minutes to work on something. We can control the spotlight of attention through the executive function of the working memory and focus on which thoughts and ideas we will let pass to be stored in our long-term memory.

We can support and strengthen our professional semantic memory. Every time we focus and concentrate, every time we give information, projects and experiences considerable, effortful thoughts, and every time we consciously evaluate and conclude, we will strengthen our professional semantic memory. Also, every time we elaborate, tell others, or repeat learned information or knowledge, we will strengthen our semantic memory. Lists help too (funny enough, as I kind of hate them). A list is something that is in an order, is short, and has a very specific intention. Our semantic memory likes order, and it likes lists. It uses the structure of the list as a memory cue.

We can develop memorable professional mental models. We organize our professional experiences, memories, and thinking in professional concepts and mental models. Concepts and mental models are therefore at the center of our professional mental life because they allow us to consolidate accumulated experiences and contexts, complexity, the view from the many, big picture knowledge into generalized representations we can grasp and remember. Mental models are remembering tools and we can practice how to develop memorable professional mental models. The five levels of professional depth and the four professional contexts are generalized and hopeful memorable mental models.

We can avoid our mental models from becoming too stable. It takes accumulated experiences to develop mental models, and these models are therefore relatively stable models we have built and used to understand and frame specific aspect of our professional knowledge and context. Because they take time to develop, they also become internalized and personal. Moreover, because we have invested time in them, they become something we defend. This is how the economy, urbanization, or wastewater treatment plants work. However, sometimes our developed mental models are wrong because we have not updated them with new experiences, conscious thoughts, or experiences from others. They especially can become wrong if the big picture, the view from the many, has changed without we noticing it. Then we are in real trouble if we think we know what we are talking about.

We can deliberately think slow. Professional thinking and knowledge work in two systems, fast and slow. The fast system provides quick solutions and decisions based on what is in memory, what is familiar, and what we believe we know. The fast system relies on cognitive shortcuts. When we make fast professional decisions or judgments, we link to these cognitive shortcuts in our fast system. With sufficient professional experience, these shortcuts provide the right answer or an answer that is good enough. However, when the shortcuts provide the wrong answer, we make biased errors. One way to overcome the harmful biases and reduce errors is to slow down and deliberate in decisions and judgments. In the slow system, professional thinking is carried out in a serial or sequential fashion, rather than in the parallel fashion used in the fast system. Sometimes we must slow down, think carefully, and use slow deduction to consider what is true or if our mental model needs updating.

We can be mindful of the fact that familiarity and experience work not so well for big picture contexts. When we make professional predictions and judgments, we take advantage of what we see, what we know, and what we remember. This, in general, works well for us in near and familiar contexts but not so well when we encounter the big picture or big data contexts, such as globalization, urbanization, or demographic transitions. Are urban areas more dangerous than rural areas? Our immediate answer to the question reflects our experience of having seen something, been told or read something, and of remembering it. The available evidence is not really wrong as it reflects what we saw or read. The problem is that it is just not always the right information to answer that big picture question.

We can be mindful of the fuzziness of our episodic professional memory. Our episodic memory is not perfect but far from it. Despite remembering a lot about a professional experience, we do not remember many of the specific details of that experience. Even after a short time of the experience, our episodic memory will be very selective in its focus and remembrance. Moreover, what we often remember is what we have retold. We remember it now because we later elaborated on it, and we use this recollection to illustrate different aspects we now find relevant. Each recollection now becomes a new episode. If we remember something slightly wrong or differently, then that becomes part of the memory. It is inevitable, and it is easy to see how our professional episodic memory becomes distorted over time. It is all but impossible to know which details were directly experienced by us when we first had the experience and how many were sort of added later.

We must be mindful of the fact that professional semantic and episodic reference points are two very different things. For our professional semantic memories what matters is the meaning in general as being too specific would be detrimental. It would not be helpful if we thought urbanization only applied to staying in Johannesburg and experiencing this city grow. Through our semantic memory system, we learn that urbanization is a general mental model that applies to all sorts of areas globally. A semantic memory (the general mental model and knowledge of urbanization) and the creation of a new episodic memory (seeing a city grow in a specific place at a specific time) are two different kinds of reference points because they are storing two different kinds of things, even though they may be related to the same original event.

We can ask and believe our metamemory. The accumulation of experience can result in overconfidence as it can make us think we already know how to undertake a new assignment or project as we have seen something very similar before. However, contexts change, uncertainties arise, emergence is a reality, and in complex professional settings we can never be certain that we know beforehand how to implement the best and most efficient solution. To stay honest, we must continuously ask our metamemory of the limits of our experience and knowledge.

From Fundamentals to Accumulations, Project Stories, and Anchors

The fundamental platforms to become professional project managers revolve around the accumulation of professional reference points, the recognition of technical, people, power, and complex unforeseen contexts, and the utilization and moderation of the spreading activation system. Dreyfus and Dreyfus were correct when they argued that the accumulation of professional reference points is critical, and they were correct that context becomes ever more important as we move up the five professional capacity levels. They, however, only defined context broadly and I have added the four professional contexts to frame and provide an additional mental model for the *contexts* that matter for project managers, for professionals. The four professional contexts give us four different *critical agendas* we need to master. We need to be able to manage the content and control agenda and be technically competent. We need to be able to manage the people agenda and be competent in communication, consultation, and team building. We need to be able to manage the political agenda and be competent in influencing, negotiating, and managing support and resistance. Moreover, we need to be able to cope with the complex emergent agenda and be competent in adapting and initiating self-organizing processes.

Dreyfus and Dreyfus showed that our professional capacity evolves over time in relation to the number of accumulated reference points and experiences. I think there is a similar evolution in our ability to recognize and internalize the four professional contexts and agendas. We start out mainly by focusing on our technical contexts and agendas and then move on to become better and better at recognizing and dealing with people first, then power, and finally complex unforeseen contexts and agendas. During our career, we get exposed to different aspects of our professional world, we accumulate and collect reference points, and slowly we begin to understand

and realize the impact the different contexts have on our achievements. And only slowly we understand and learn how to operate within and balance the different technical, people, power, and complex unforeseen agendas.

The five levels and the four contexts are integrated, parallel, and concurrent and provide us with an insightful mental model to understand, assess, and develop our professional capacity. If we want to get better at what we do, we need to be able to internalize, integrate, and balance our understanding of professional capacity levels in relation to the four contexts. Any professional's capacity, any professional project story, and any decision taken or lesson learned must be understood in relation to this professional matrix. We need to be able to honestly access our own and others' capacity levels in relation to the actual professional experiences accumulated in relation to the four contexts and agendas. Does the capacity of my team combined have sufficient capacities in relation to the professional agendas? Do I have team members with deep technical experience and does the team have enough political capacity to manage the political agenda?

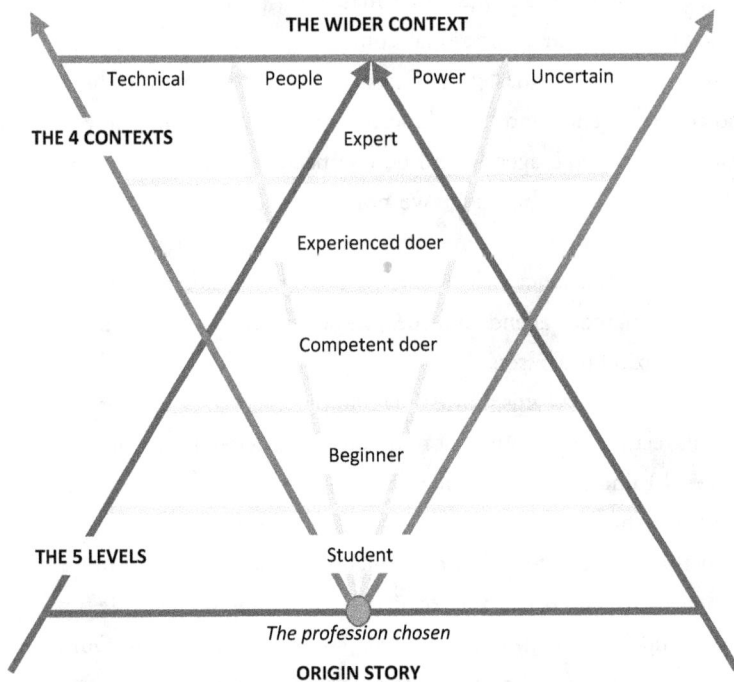

The Professional Capacity Matrix

The Professional Capacity Matrix illustrates the four factors leading to professional capacity. The starting point is our personal *origin story*, our early years, that ends with our selection of a profession and the area we want to be professional in. Our professional capacity level then becomes the combined result of the *accumulation of reference points* (the pyramid) and our ability to recognize and deal with the *four professional TPPU (technical, people, power, unforeseen) contexts and agendas* (the inverted pyramid). However, we are always *anchored* in a wider context, in organizations, sectors, economies, and demographics. And we must understand this wider context as it directly impacts our professional capacity, it provides us with opportunities and constraints, and it tells us what to expect. Origin stories, reference point accumulation, TPPU contexts, and the wider context are the four critical factors that give us our project management capacity, our professionalism.

The first of the four factors, our origin story, was discussed and reflected upon in Chapter 1. The other three factors are covered in the next three chapters.

CHAPTER 3

Accumulation of Reference Points

Reminding, based on the examination of an internal library of professional reference points or experiences, each with different contexts, is what enables learning and is the basis of professional capacity. To be reminded of relevant prior professional reference points, we create those reference points subconsciously by thinking about them or telling someone about them.[1] Then, again subconsciously, we label the previously experienced reference points in some way. No one ever teaches us how to do this. No one teaches us how to label professional reference points or retrieve reference points from our memory. Yet, our entire professional ability depends on this capability. We need to see something as an instance of something we have seen before, to make a judgment about it and learn from it. The more reference points we have in our internal library of reference points, the more professional we can act.

The importance of this accumulation of reference points and contextual variation is the focus of this chapter and three key issues are highlighted. We must consider how we, during our career, jobs, and projects, develop a path that allows us to accumulate not only reference points but also variations in contexts. *Count your reference points and build a career* that focuses on context variation and platforms is my advice. Then, we must know which reference points accumulated gives us our professionalism and not be distracted by reference points that will not make us think and act professional. Collect and *focus on the normal reference points* is in my experience the best starting point. And finally, we must accumulate not only our own reference points but reference points from other professionals, and for this, we have no way around but to *read* and educate ourselves throughout to add reference points to our own experience-based reference points. These three paths to accumulation of professional reference points are discussed next.

Accumulation 1: Count Your Reference Points and Build a Career

When we start out on a professional career, we do not think too much on how slowly to accumulate contextual knowledge and reference points. When I finished university, I wanted to be an international development expert; helping the poor was a bit of an obsession. But then, my university professor, Peter Kragh Jespersen, offered me to colecture with him on strategic management, power, and organization theory. I agreed and stayed within the university bubble the first year after graduation. But teaching has never really been my thing. I am not good at it, and I started to look for something else. After many job applications, first naively only for international positions, then national ministries and big co-operations, and finally and humbly also to municipalities, I got a position at Copenhagen municipality as an organizational consultant, which was what I in fact had studied! A couple of years after I started, I read a study of what we think is important for our first job. Before we start, we focus on the meaning and type of work and organization we want to work for, for example, the United Nations, Google, and Apple; we want to make a positive impact on the world; we want to get somewhere fast. Interestingly, when asked again two years after starting the first job, everyone said the only thing that really matters is who our boss is and how good or bad he or she is. The thing about meaning or impact on the world is suddenly forgotten. Luckily, I got Kurt Pedersen as my first boss, and he was a real pleasure to work for. The message, clear and simple, get started, cross our finger for a good boss and then put our full heart into the assignments we are allocated, and never mind how boring they might look. At least, our first collection of reference points and context-specific knowledge has begun, and we are on our way.

Document experiences in projects. Through our career, we should count our experiences as these are the most valuable we have as professionals. And we shall document these experiences, and the CV is the place for that. Unfortunately, CVs often do not do that. They just document where we worked with what in general. In my experience, the best way to document our work is to divide our work into projects and document all projects we have been involved in, responsible for or manager of. A project is a thing that has a start and an end. In documenting our work, we shall not focus on results, but just focus on the activities and projects completed. Not more than four to five lines per project, short, objectively, and to the point. What did I do? Start this practical documentation from our first job and continue throughout our career and we have a good base description of our experiences, things done, and, thereby, also indirectly of our capabilities, just by documenting what projects and work assignments we have been involved in. Facts are facts. Experience convinces and impresses when they are documented. Put numbers on as much as possible. We can, in the CV, play a bit with semantics, especially in the first years where our experiences are slightly thin, but never lie. It is my experience that we often take this documentation of our capabilities steaming from our experience too lightly, which is strange as this list of what we have done professionally and experienced is the core of our professional capabilities.

The three in 10-year rule. When asked, I always say that, in the first 10 years of our career, we should have three different jobs. Now why is that? That is what I did; so I rationalize it and that is likely part of it. But also, and in the context of this book, it makes sense as it is important that we, in the beginning of our career, gather and get experience with variation, different contexts, and different types of complex work settings. We start out not knowing too much and, in the first decade of our career, we need to change and shift context. We need exposure and practice in working in different contexts and the earlier in our career we get variation in context under our skin, the better.

The four-year rule. Throughout my career, I have experienced a rather peculiar thing that has applied to all my positions, even the last one where I now work for myself as an entrepreneur. The first year in a new job, we are pretty much useless. We do not know the setting, the agendas, the context, the networks, the games, our place, and all the other things so important for being effective or just useful. We fumble. The second year, we start to get a better grab of things, our established networks start to work for us, and we start to understand the context and are finding our feet. The third year, we take off and real productivity, results, and impact happen. This is the year where we really are valuable for our boss and the organization as we know how to fit in and produce outputs that have value and impact. This is often the year where we work like mad because the demand and needs for our inputs are high. In the fourth year, we start to know almost too much about the context, colleagues, and internal power games and repetition unavoidably creeps in. Habituation and boredom set in, and with that comes a bit of tiredness, lack of motivation and innovation, a lapse in energy and inputs, and therefore also in outputs and impact. This cycle supports the three in 10-year rule. We should not leave too often and never before the end of year three as then we would not have gained the valuable experiences in the important third year. And we should not stay too long after year four for the opposite reasons. I have experienced in all positions I have had that my energy and motivation increase until the third year and fall from year four, where after I have had to adjust, innovate, change, and jump—which I have done every three to four years during my whole career.

The three-in-one year rule. In all our jobs, from the first to the last, it is key to stand out, achieve, be memorable, and not become too much part of the furniture. This is easier said than done because it applies to both when we are underused and undervalued and when we are busy, valued, and in there. One way to not get swallowed by the day-to-day churn, the repetitions, and the boss' constant immediate and always urgent demands and tasks is to set the simple goal of achieving our own three memorable yearly targets. I have tried to practice this rule, and I have normally judged my achievements against the grandmother method; at the end of the year, I imagine how I would tell my grandmother in few sentences the three things I have achieved this year, achievements that, maybe, would make her proud. Again, this sounds easier than it is because we are always part of a bigger setting and part of interlinked complex process with many actions and actors, and this often makes our own inputs and results a bit blurry. But we must set our own targets and we must stand out just a little. And here the ability for story telling becomes key. We must have good, convincing, and simple stories to tell, year in, year out.

Always leave before we think the time is right. Because shifts and changes are so important for getting contextual professional experience, we must also be good at leaving. After any three- or four-year work period, we have built an experience platform and can and should be ready to transit again. I think the key here is to always leave before we think the time is right. New job applications and the search for new opportunities shall start before we feel the time is right and when we are most comfortable and in our best gear and year, as this is the best time to gamble, to apply for positions and opportunities we feel maybe are a bit above our level. This is the time when we have nothing to lose and all to win. The worse time to look for new opportunities is when we are struggling, tired of our boss, or running out of steam, creativity, or innovations. The worst time, of course, is when we have been asked to leave. Each time we move, we need a reference, and the best reference is usually the boss.

Grow the career by changing organizational context. I find that we should grow our career by regularly changing our organizational context. To look for promotion within the ranks is fine and, if it happens, good. The problem is that it takes our focus away from the need for contextual knowledge accumulation and instead makes us focus on the internal power and reputational games played in any organization of professionals. These internal games are generally not worth playing. Many studies have shown that we are very good at social stratification and seldom get it wrong. Place 20 professionals in a workplace and they will within a short time have stratified each other quite precisely, who is best, second, and so on. We do not even have to worry about this, and I seldom understand why there is so much focus and gossip around this as it comes automatically to us. This is, by the way, also the reason I find we should never ask for performance or salary increases. If our boss or organization is not able to stratify and reward thereafter, we have the wrong boss or are in the wrong organization and should leave as quickly as possible. If we aim to grow our career, the fastest and best way is to leave and get a higher or better position somewhere else. And when we have left, we have left. The social dynamics of complex professional workplaces are so intense and absorbing that no one really has time for the ones who left. Do not go back to get help or hope to get a contract because we worked so well together. It does not work like that. And do not make the mistake I made once: after having been outstationed for four years, I came back to the same organization to start the same job I previously had—a disaster. "Stick to the change and transition" is good formula and we should be fine. Change is good because context is key, especially later in our professional life. I have received a good dose of contextual change, reference points, and variation during my career. I have made career transitions from academic lecturer, government bureaucrat, diplomat, and Danish management specialist to global development consultant and entrepreneur. I am beginning to feel I have been contextual vaccinated.

Shift to moving from platform to platform. After around a decade of opportunistic or accidental professional experience and context accumulation, it is my experience that we should change from "change is good in itself" to "getting from platform to platform." At some stage, we have developed professional platforms of experience within certain professional fields of competence. As it takes time to develop professional platforms, and as time is running, we cannot continue to start all over, we must begin to look at what we have in our professional bag, and we must utilize and optimize this baggage. If we have 15 years of project management, electrical engineering, or medical experience, we need to build on that as it has become a part of us, of our reference points; it has become our professional platform from where we must develop and excel. And there will, whether we like it or not, be ever more we cannot realistically become professional at. We cannot, late in our career, become a level-four professional bridge engineer, doctor, architect, or whatever we have not gained decades of experience in. If we aim to become good professionals, we must accept that to become good at something, we need to gain experience-based contextual professional knowledge. And then we must also accept that as time goes by, doors do close behind us. We, at this later stage in our career, probably for the first time, need some strategy or direction. With the platforms I had built over the first part of my career (consultancy, big company employment, global networks, and project management), I chose to go entrepreneurial, to leave the salaried safety net behind, and try it on my own.

Accumulation 2: Focus on the Normal Reference Points

I have been involved in 225 projects and I went through them all to look at the numbers to see if there were any patterns of interest. The projects

I have been responsible for have followed the 80/20 Pareto principle; 80 percent, or 193 projects, were projects that involved the development of strategies, policies, plans, feasibility studies, designs, and technical and financial assessments. Paperwork projects. Thinking analytical and strategic. The requirement being structured in my mind. The 20 percent, or 29 projects, were projects that involved the construction and implementation of physical stuff; building agro-villages; installing solar water heaters, biogas facilities, and PV solar plant; or replacing light bulbs. Physical projects. Planning activities, controlling construction teams. The requirement being structured on the ground. Why Pareto sneaked in here I do not know, but this distribution at least gives some indication of the width of my experiences and capacity. Based on my experience profile, ask me to be team leader for some analytical professional stuff and we will be fine. Ask me to build something and maybe a second opinion is appropriate.

But more importantly, the look at the many showed some other interesting distributions: 92 percent of professional projects are normal projects with approximate intended results, 5 percent become successes that create results and impacts beyond the project scope, and the remaining 3 percent fail miserably and embarrass us. In their implementation, 95 percent encounter normal project resistance and frictions but are otherwise implemented pretty much as planned, while 5 percent encounter serious problems and are really hard to implement. How do I know? I don't. But that is how my 225 projects turned out. I would not be able to explain the methodology I used, but trust me, I know my projects. I know which ones failed, which one were normal or succeeded beyond expectations, and which ones for different reasons were difficult to implement.

We all have our own professional experiences, but what I can conclude from what I have experienced is that if we act professionally, then most projects, interactions, and results, in hindsight and in the majority, will be normal. Of all my projects, I assess that 92 percent, or 204, had results and impacts pretty much as planned and to the general satisfaction of the ones involved, the funder, the beneficiaries, the recipients, the stakeholders, my bosses. This means that in these projects, technical, people, power, and unforeseen aspect were balanced; dilemmas kept in check; and results reached satisfactory. Not more, not less. For our professionalism. the normal implemented project is King. We learn from the normal, the repetitive, the average, but well-implemented project. We learn from patterns we can recognize in the next project. My own professionalism stems from these 204 projects: how to design, implement, assess, balance, judge, and decide to get good enough project results and impacts. My next project will be normal and average, and I am good with that. I am a professional that just wants to implement professionally what is in front of me.

I have learned something from failures, but not in the way many popular quotes go: "Success is stumbling from failure to failure with no loss of enthusiasm" (Winston Churchill) or "it is fine to celebrate success, but it is more important to heed the lessons of failure" (Bill Gates). Unfortunately, or fortunately, that is not how professional life works. Depressing failures are there in our accumulated experience box, but they are not the foundation of accumulated professional experience or the key to become professional. We learn and become professional from the many, not the few. If most of our projects fail, something is likely very wrong, and we have learned too little to become a professional. Would I have liked to have avoided my seven failed projects? Of course, and I would have been pretty much the same professional without. Could I have avoided them? Likely not, as that is also not how life works. It is unlikely that we will go through our professional career without some technical, people, power, or complex unforeseen induced failures. We must be able to deal and live with these failures. I have documented one of these failures, the wicked Tshwane Food and Energy Center, in detail on my homepage.[2]

Of my projects, 213, or 95 percent, were implemented pretty much as planned. In these projects, it was possible to manage the normal implementation problems and the issues that projects encounter. It was possible to solve and balance the technical, people, power, and complex unforeseen issues that popped up along the way. Nothing in the implementation process proved to be too difficult, hard, or complicated to stop these projects from reaching their planned outputs and results. Similar to the projects that create normal results, these normal implemented projects are also the ones we learn the most from and get our professional implementation skills from—how to juggle technical issues, expectations, changes, and the unforeseen and still get there.

The average is normally boring, while, as outliers or exceptions, impactful successes and depressing failures are much more interesting.

They take up more space in our memory, in literature, and in our stories. I remember my few impactful successes and failures very well, but because they are both personal and outliers, I have placed them all on my home-page.[3] You are welcome to take a look; there might even be some lessons in there somewhere.

A simple counting and structuring of the many, of all projects I have been involved in, gave me some interesting patterns and insights into results and implementation and how it was the normal and boring that had made me a professional. And it made me think of results, success, and impact. On the most fundamental level, processes are nonrepeatable. You cannot step into the same river twice. I have found that this simple fact should guide our mental model for success. We work hard and aim for success all the time, but success is a nonrepeatable, fickle, mental thing. It is in our head.

If we were successful, this success is not easy to simply repeat. We have to start all over every time to achieve success again. That is difficult to accept. Even though I have been involved in hundreds of projects, I am still surprised by the complexity surrounding each of them. Each time I have started a new project, it has almost felt like starting all over. Some things have looked similar, and this, of course, helps, but a key task has always been to learn and understand the specific setting for any new project: the people involved; the internal power games; the specific obsta-cles and opportunities; and the details so important to gain results and impact. And each time, this getting-to-know has been energy consuming. Similar to the feeling, I think, everybody has when we start a new job: not knowing who to ask, who is in and who is out, and not fully knowing how to behave. This means we are always a bit nervous and insecure— and should be, as having professional capacity depends on being sensi-tive to the actual context. Which technical approach is most suited right now in this setting? Which people to involve to gain maximum impact? Which coalitions to make? For these judgments, there is no cookbook. Creation of success and results requires balanced professional assessments, judgments, decisions, and actions.

There is no doubt that professional achievements are much more than the preparation of a plan, the allocation of a budget, and an activity and time schedule. Successful achievements are about being able to work and implement in complex, changing settings—about understanding and acknowledging real-life difficulties, complexities, and paradoxes that surround any project, effort, or achievement. Creating results and success is about pinpointing which issues should be balanced, about making thoughtful judgments, and then acting, seeing what happens and readjusting—about being able to simultaneously balance participation and processes to achieve results; about the simultaneous use of front- and backstage activities; and about the simultaneous use of creativity, innovation, flexibility, and still getting somewhere.

Whether we succeed in all of this is a matter of which definition we use. Success is never a clear one-dimensional thing or achievement. Success is achievements of predetermined goals, but goals and goalposts move. I work hard to become richer, but when have I arrived? I work hard to get my projects from A to B, but when I am at B, I always find that something went fine but something did not go fully to plan. I created jobs, but some people complained. I prepared the policy, but too fast with too little involvement. Which aspect we focus on in the end will determine how successful we will find ourselves and our projects. The feeling of success is in the head. My brother went through a tough period, where he had to teach himself to zero-start every day—making the first good morning cup of coffee the first success achievement of the day and from there dividing each day into tiny success stories in order to get through the day. I constantly push the envelope, constantly get involved in new projects, constantly expect new and bigger achievements, and, for many decades, forgot to enjoy the successes I made. I forgot, or did not know, how to define success in my head.

I have slowly learned that what matters and gives pleasure is not so much visible results and successes, but it is professional confidence. And that is what repetition brings and that is what can be repeated. I have learned to trust that when I know something I know it. I now know I have a number of these professional areas: project management, how to close a contract, the likelihood of success when we start a process, an advanced bullshit detector, and a good feel of when things likely will go nowhere. Besides the depth of my experience, one of my strengths and the source of my professional confidence has been the width of my professional exposure. My strength is that I have come to cover all four areas.

Technically I can think, structure, and write rationally; I can balance people; I know how to recognize and deal with power; and I have experienced complexity throughout. This professional confidence means that I know I can move to a new job in a new country I have never been to before, where I know nobody and have a professional network of zero, as was the situation when I moved to South Africa, and still know that I will make it. I am focused and driven, I get things done, I set plans and direction, I pursue, and I am busy and immersed in what I do. I am an energy field that burns for what I am doing right here and now.

And what about the impact of all the efforts and energy I have put into all these projects? After having studied, taught, and stopped being interested in philosophy, in Camus, Sartre, and existentialism, I read Frank Wilczek's inspiring *Fundamentals, Ten Keys to Reality*, a physic book about our fundamentals, and he made me think of what matters and what not. He writes:

> *According to our present best understanding, the primary properties of matter, from which all other properties can be derived, are these three:*
>
>
>
> *Mass*
> *Charge*
> *Spin*
>
>
>
> *That's it.*[4]

That made me think. Mass, charge, spin—that is all there is. That is how everything works. Atoms, electrons, nucleus, protons, and neutrons. How the universe works. How matter works. Mass, charge, spin. The parallels to our life, private and professional, dawned on me. We are born as matter, we are charged, we gain experience, and then we start to spin. It is not mass, charge, aim, and fly like an arrow. There is no particular direction, just spinning. On we go, like a gyroscope; we become an energy field, a temporary force field. All we need to do is to charge and spin and then we will impact others in our force field. No direction, just impacting the ones around us. We are not here to impact through the specifics we achieve, through the results or success of our projects, and through the plan or strategy we follow. We spin. And we pass on energy and reference points.

Accumulation 3: Read

We always need to add knowledge to our own experiences and reference points, and one way, likely the best way, we can add to our own experiences is by reading. Our professional base is our own professional experiences but, to this, we need to continuously add what we can read and learn from others. Only then do our mature professional capacities have a chance to get sufficient width. By reading, we add insights from people who have studied and documented specific issues and contexts in a systemic manner on an accumulated level, the level from the many, the levels we do not have insight into from an individual experience-base or do not see from our own standpoint because we are in the middle of it all.

I still clearly remember my high school teacher telling me that I should not worry if I did not understand what I read. He said subconsciously it will accumulate and, the next time I read something similar, it would be a little bit easier to understand; my reference points would have accumulated and changed my capacity to understand. I think I have made him proud as I have read plenty of books I did not understand. I read David Deutsch's *The Beginning of Infinity*[5] from start to end and practically did not understand a word: just sitting there reading, hoping something would accumulate!

Recently my daughter asked me why we must read so much. She might have been thinking of herself and why I always ask her to read more, but what do I know. She had just started as junior consultant in a large global consulting company. My immediate working memory answer was that otherwise she would have no computer to write on or no bridges to cross. All knowledge, how to build a bridge or how to understand the brain, is stored in books, and if we want to continue to progress, we have no options but to read them. But then my memory with all its spreading activation took over and I moved from the why to the how. The general question of why was followed by plugging into the experience-based mental models I have developed and stored for how to gain knowledge and information quickly and effectively. And I held an unprepared lecture on how she, in the position she had, should read. And suddenly an hour had passed.

By the way, this was some of my spreading-activated speaking notes. When we enter a new area—global consultants enter new settings all the time—we need to quickly get hold of two levels of context. She had been assigned to a project that over two years should create knowledge sharing between professionals in five global cities. She had no experience in the field whatsoever and my advice went like this: First, get a hold of the project context. Google design and evaluation of networking projects between cities; go through the first 10 Google pages; and download the 15 best and most relevant reports and evaluations (filter for source reliability). Then I old-fashionedly said print them, read them carefully, make notes, and summarize them into your own understanding of the content, opportunities, issues, and problems in global cities networking projects. I am certain this will give a very good feel of what this specific field is about (and provide some good buzzwords). Second, get a hold of the general context. For global networking of urban professionals, this would include understanding better the general context of globalization, demography, urbanization, and levels of economic development. I suggested four books that would quickly give her a good frame for these issues. I think she found this overwhelming, but if she wanted to become an asset to her project manager, she had no way around getting a feel of the project and its general context. I doubt she followed my advice; her contract was not renewed, but she will be fine and will, like everybody else, gain her own experiences, including the experience of not taking advice from an experienced global consultant professional.

But, like her, I also sometimes did not read and then had to accept that no spreading activation takes place. I was called for the final interview for a job as country director in Kenya for a large international institution. I was still in my job as a global project manager, flying all over the world from project to project. A mix of this busy-ness and misguided confidence (this was my field) meant I did not prepare well for the interview. Halfway through the interview, one of the interviewers asked me to describe the landscape in Kenya: Was it flat or did it have mountains? My metamemory superfast told me that I had no clue of the landscape in Kenya, while my semantic or episodic memories frantically scrambled to try to find some connections to something somewhere. But no spreading activation happened, my metamemory won, and I did not get the job. Fair enough. I forgot to read.

CHAPTER 4

Accumulation of TPPU Reference Points

The importance of our technical, people, power, and complex unforeseen (TPPU) professional context and agendas is the focus of this chapter. The chapter entails six paths that improve our ability to manage professional with TPPU contexts and agendas. It begins with two general paths that make us deal better with TPPU context and agendas, *accumulate deep project experiences* and *juggle the four implementation agendas*, and continues with more specific paths to deal with different aspects of the four TPPU agendas; *make plans; expand your professional network; deal with power games; use numbers and logic; think in levels; and recognize short, long, and hidden patterns.* The chapter does not go in any detail with the common recommended paths to become better professional project managers—the technical and people project management skills (plenty of other books for that)—but gives attention to the more complicated paths, the paths that requires us to balance complexities and contexts.

Before I get to these six TPPU paths, here is a project story to kick start the chapter. Projects give us a chance to develop professional *depth* as they expose us to real-life TPPU contexts and agendas, and accumulation of projects we have managed is the base unit for making us experienced project managers. I have been involved in 225 projects and could write 225 professional dense project stories with hundreds of different actors set in 24 different cultural locations around the world. I will not do that. I will, however, in this book go in depth with three of these 225 projects. The three professional projects are ones I was engulfed in for a long time, long enough to give me a good professional grasp of content and context. Technically, the projects concern the implementation of a technocratic environmental management system, the construction of a new wastewater treatment system, and the entrepreneurial planning of renewable energy facilities. The projects are my own experience-based projects from Borneo, Thailand, and South Africa.

Each of us has our own projects that has given us depth and made us good at what we do. I have selected these three projects because they are projects that gave me depth in relation to complicated professional topics, agendas, and contexts, and they provided me with professional project management lessons I think others can learn from. The first shows how implementation of apparently simple but unavoidable technical systems is linked closely with critical TPPU issues. The second underlines the importance of context and of getting the contextual up-against's right. When we fail, it is often because we misunderstand the context that surrounds us. And the third links complexities of evolution, differentiations, and specialization to the apparent simple issue of making and executing a strategic plan. The three projects show important problems and balances all project managers face and underline critical aspects of professional TPPU depth.

Good project stories are shorthand for a lot of information that was digested in the process, leading to the lessons learned and the abstract mental models the stories bring forward. Our written language, unfortunately, is rudimentary compared to the depth of our professional experiences and the complexities, paradoxes, balances, processes, and judgments they entail. We, as professionals, have available and are caught in stories, humor, unsolvable situations, paradoxes, backstage power, politics, corruption, people liked or disliked, all the things so important, but at the same time so difficult to convey with the type of written language. I could, like a good novel by Joseph Conrad when he succeeds in describing human subtleties and ambiguities, try to describe the projects as impressionistic stories to capture real-life professional depth and complexities, but it should be clear by now that I am no Conrad, so sadly, in this book, you will find no brilliant impressionistic project descriptions. But as professional reference points, based on having been involved long and deep in a project and its context, are so central to becoming good at what we do, they are our deep contextual reference points, and they give us depth, I have no option but to warn you, give it a go, and hope for the best. The first project story follows next, the others later in the book.

Project Story 1: Implementing a Technocratic System on Borneo—Juggling Professional Agendas

Datuk Eric Juin, Dr Tony Greer, Carsten H. Laugesen

I worked and lived on the island of Borneo for four years. We had won a project to capacity develop the Sabah State Department of Environment and I was seconded by the Danish Government and my company as the chief technical advisor (CTA), responsible for the project and a technical team of 35 international and national long- and short-term experts.

At 39, I was a young CTA, but at least I had come to realize that this thing about professional capacity, whether organizational or individual, was a complicated matter, and the mental model of the four different types of professional capacity had already taken shape in my mind. The international capacity development projects I had evaluated or been involved in had all used simplistic, technical approaches to professional capacity. We need these technical skills; someone must teach us and then we will be fine. I knew I could do better.

The Plan

I had not been involved in my company's proposal and knew my chance to put my thoughts on professional capacity development into action lay in the inception period. I also knew that if this external international assistance-funded project should have a chance to get any foothold, it had to link to the main responsibility areas of the department, and it should involve and benefit all professional officers in the department.

The director of the department, Eric Juin, the deputy Yabi Yangkat, internal work groups, and I planned in the inception period that the project should have six components: environmental policy, environmental planning, environmental impact assessment (EIA), environmental monitoring and enforcement, environmental management information systems, and administration. These areas linked the project closely to all the main sections, tasks, and responsibilities of the department.

We defined the main implementation approach as development of strategies, action plans, manuals, guidelines, and working procedures and, based on these, develop, link, and implement specific training, network, and pilot activities. A total of 26 outputs were planned and to these were linked 86 specific activities to be implemented.

The way objectives, outputs, and activities were planned and formulated followed the typical logical framework approach (LFA)—rational and straightforward. Where I tried to innovate was in the way we applied and integrated the four professional capacity approaches to the department and its officers. In addition to the traditional technical outputs, such as handbooks, manuals, and procedures, we added training (people), networking (power), and piloting (emergence) outputs. Training outputs were linked to each of the six areas to strengthen participation and consisted of tailor-made training packages and participation in external training and conference activities whenever opportunities arose. It was decided that the project should withhold a lump sum for implementation of emergent networking opportunities as they unfolded during the four-year project. Pilot outputs were described as open-ended experiments of new ways of doing things.

I never mentioned and we never discussed my four-context mental model for professional capacity development. Nudging and making sense did the trick. Taken one by one, none of the 26 outputs or 86 activities was special or exceptional. Taken together, they were, from the outset, my attempt at setting the scene for an integrated approach to organizational and professional capacity development. I held outputs clear and verifiable, and in the formulation of activities to reach these outputs included processes that would take us into networking, experiments, and piloting.

After the one-month inception period, the project design was agreed by all key internal and external stakeholders and implementation could start.

The Implementation

The area that had the most attention was without doubt the EIA area. This was the area the director was most interested in, the area where the department had direct and real legal power, and the area that had the most political and stakeholder attention. The EIA component had 6 outputs and 32 activities planned. We were to develop and implement a new EIA system in the state with clear powers and responsibilities.

The EIA system is an assessment and approval system, where proponents of development activities are obliged by law to submit to the environmental department an EIA report before commencing with the activities. These activities are called the prescribed activities and are listed in the environmental law, such as specified sized forestry or agriculture activities or construction of roads, hotels, bridges, and buildings. The project proponent hires an environmental consultant to undertake the EIA study. The department will review the submitted information and then either approve, with or without conditions, or not approve the proposed project. This EIA system makes environmental departments all over the world very powerful.

The first thing we did was to establish a team of EIA officers, myself and my deputy Tony Greer. This team started by studying all EIA reports submitted earlier. This turned out to be a relatively easy task as there were only few submissions in the three years since the EIA system had been established. These reports were general, theoretical, and clearly cut-and-paste from environmental textbooks. They had almost no information or data from the actual site, which were often incorrect and said nothing about which environmental mitigation measures should be in place, by who, for how much, or paid by who. They were undertaken by consultants trying to please their customer, the project proponents, and get by as easily as possible. All had been approved. The review showed a need for a major overhaul of the EIA system. This was not professional. On that, all agreed. And in a state with plenty of developmental activities, the EIA system basically was not applied.

The team then studied EIA regulations from around the world. In the Internet age, it is possible to sit on a remote island and, within few days, screen and compare a huge number of different international environmental laws and EIA systems. It was not that the old EIA system and regulations were particularly poor. The system in fact looked like many other EIA systems. But some countries had tried to improve and innovate. The planned project output was to produce a General Handbook on EIA Policy and Procedures, but the director found that we needed to be ambitious and add to the handbook the drafting and submission of a new state environmental law. I agreed. We got ideas, inspiration, adjusted, added, and came up with a proposed new environmental law for the State Assembly to approve. The law included new procedures and powers and provided for a dramatic change of the EIA system in the state. I found that the existing law included too many prescribed activities, but the director wanted to keep the same long list of development activities that should be EIA approved. He was the director, so he won that argument.

The proposed revised law was sent to hearing to all relevant stakeholders, governmental agencies, associations, and NGOs. Minor adjustments were made and then it was sent to the State Assembly for approval. With the help of the newly appointed chief minister, we got the new environmental law approved in the first year of the project. We could now start to plan and detail the new EIA system and processes.

The EIA system is a traditional bureaucratic system requiring transparency, predictability, and clear systems for workflows, decision making, and follow-up. System management was therefore the first we had to look at: who should do what and when. The director wanted the department to become ISO 9000 certified to systematize and standardize the EIA system. Even though this also was not a project output, I again agreed. After months of tedious work on development of manuals and workflow descriptions, intensive training of officers in system requirements, audits, and examinations, the ISO 9000 certification was received, the first in the state for a public administration. We had a new law enacted by the State Assembly and an ISO 9000 certification in place in little over a year. The department, the director, and the project looked good.

We now moved to the development of guidelines and regulations for selected key prescribed activities: river sand and stone extraction, hill excavations, hill slope constructions, forestry, agriculture, livestock farming, and quarrying. We wanted to produce new guidelines for environmental consultants on how to write the EIA reports—which key information they should include to describe impacts. Also, they should not only describe impacts but also propose practical mitigation measures and include costs, deadlines, and responsibilities for these measures. And we wanted to produce new procedures for approvals. Approvals should not only be a yes or no (a no we had never seen) but focus more on mitigation measures and include these in the approval conditions with clear follow-up procedures. I found that if the EIA system should benefit the environment, it would mainly be through proper, appropriate, and justifiable mitigation measures.

What should have been a rather straightforward technical exercise became everything but. We, especially my deputy Tony Greer and I, attacked the issue of technical guidelines. First, we got surprised that the Google method we had used to find good environmental policies did not produce much. It was easy to find plenty of policies, objectives, and strategies, but almost impossible to find practical how-to EIA assessment methods. How, in practice, are we to assess and mitigate the environmental impact of river sand and stone extraction, hill excavations, hill slope constructions, forestry, or quarrying? I was stunned. Here we had a global industry, thousands of environmental impact regulations, EIA officers, and EIA consultants, but the technical standards and methods were missing.

With Tony by my side, an experienced environmental expert that had lived and worked with environmental issues on Borneo for more than a decade, we worked hard to get it right. We drafted specific prescribed activity guidelines, but we did not get to where we wanted: clear and specific guidelines for how to assess the impact of the selected prescribed activities, and then for how to mitigate the assessed adverse environmental impacts. For some prescribed activities, we could define how to assess the impacts but not come up with what to do. For most prescribed activities, we could neither.

Take construction on hill slopes. A developer has received approval from town council that he can build on that piece of land, which normally was next to many other pieces of land already developed but could not go ahead before the EIA had been approved. The general impacts we knew were soil erosion and clocking of rivers and coastal areas. This is a serious problem not only in Borneo, but worldwide. Look at a Google map of the coastal areas around Kota Kinabalu: large brown plumbs of soil runoffs reaching kilometers into the sea, killing coastal ecosystems and coral reefs. Or go inland to the beautiful but brown Kinabatangan River in eastern Sabah. We knew the overall negative impacts. But EIA is not about general impacts. It is about calculating and assessing impacts for specific development projects and telling the developer how to mitigate site-specific impacts. Soil erosion impacts happen during rain. To calculate the impact from a specific site, we need to know the amount of land exposed to soil erosion, the timing and duration of the construction period, the amount of rain falling during the construction period, the gradients, the soil composition, the runoff locations and destinations, the sensitivity of the receiving waters, and so on. This became an impossible task to calculate in praxis. Rough rules of thumb became our only way out, but not good.

The rule of thumb at least gave us a theoretical tonnage of soil leaving the disturbed piece of land, and we could move on to mitigation measures. The literature gave suggestions, and they were poor. The key mitigation suggested was the establishment of sedimentation ponds at the discharge points. In practice, this is impossible. Let us say we know the discharge points, which is surprisingly difficult in tropical locations with strong but short downpours (or we could, theoretically and at a high cost, build runoff structures directing the water to these discharge points). We then need to calculate the sizing of the sedimentation ponds. Most of the rainfall in a month falls within a couple of hours, so the ponds should be able to trap the water from these heavy rains to mitigate soil erosion and discharge into rivers. We calculated that this normally would result in the ponds becoming larger than the total development site. Add the calculation of time for sedimentation to happen, which depends on a vast number of factors, and the problems become even bigger. Sedimentation ponds were clearly not the solution, and we did not include it in our guideline. We proposed the planting of grass—not perfect, but at least something, but not something that we could calculate and assess our way to; just common sense and the formulation of a few simple rules for grass planting as quickly as possible after the soil had been disturbed.

We encountered the same fundamental assessment and mitigation problems for most of the other prescribed activities. Where we got closest was livestock farming as a prescribed activity. If we want to build a pig farm with 200 pigs, the environmental impacts are easy to calculate, and it is easy to specify the mitigation measures that should be put in place. But then the question arises: If the impacts and mitigation measures are clear, why do we need to undertake a complicated and costly EIA procedure for every new pig farm? If they are proposed on approved agricultural land, why not just tell the farmer what to do. This should be covered by regulations, not EIAs. Because of these technical how-to problems, I slowly became a strong opponent of the EIA system, not only in Borneo but everywhere. The system does not make sense. The reasons for its continued applications shall be found not in its effectiveness but in the power it gives environmental departments, its ministers and directors, and the large and powerful environmental influence industry.

All these technicalities did not worry the department or the director too much. We produced the guidelines and the department adopted them and got them printed as governmental guidelines. I could feel difficulties ahead.

During the second year, we had to secure that a group of officers not only were competent and involved in the development of the system, but also felt responsible for its implementation. The director gave the implementation of the EIA system top priority, and he assigned the best officer as team leader for a group of officers. For these officers, we implemented training and attachment programs and best practice visits to Denmark and Taiwan. With the ISO system, a good team leader, a new law, manuals and guidelines, commitment, motivation, training, political backing, and strong top management support in place, all felt the department had the technical competence to manage the system, and the new EIA system in the state took off.

From having to process fewer than five EIA reports per year, within few months, the department went to process 15 EIA reports per month. The department and the system came under pressure, and I started to notice flaws in the system. Some project developers and EIA consultants came informally and questioned the new system and procedures. We were able to process and approve more EIA reports, but the costs on their side grew and the environmental impact on the ground remained modest, if not nonexistent. I was told that the department and minister used the many new applications to gain financial advantages. The approvals were bought. After an initial improvement in the quality of the submitted EIA reports, the quality quickly started to fall back to the previous low standards. I was inexperienced in these informal financial transaction matters; I could just see that the system we had worked so hard for during the last year did not have the intended or hoped-for impact.

I started to realize that the reason for the few EIA reports submitted before I arrived was the lack of power of the department. Project developers shall apply to the local districts, and these shall then pass the developer on to the department. The local districts did not do this, and the department did not have the political strength to force them. Output five, the development of local district guidelines for environmental screening, was proposed by the director in the inception period. It was now I realized why. We selected pilot districts and established working groups with local authorities and district offices and they joined our study tours. This brought the department closer to the decisions makers in the districts, and, together with the increased reputation and visibility of the department, and likely a good amount of political wheeling and dealing, some of the districts began to pass developers on to the department, and we saw the sudden raise in applications and approvals.

I think we all recognized the project went well and was a success inside and outside the department. We got things done. The director was happy; I was happy. I liked him very much. Every day, at 12 o'clock, he passed by my office, said let's go, and we went down to the corner restaurant to have a long lunch together—Nasi Goreng and rice. We became friends in the way of just enjoying each other's company, not really taking about anything, and never department politics; he was the boss and we just sat there, eating our Nasi Goreng. I knew I had to do something with the EIA issue, but I did not know what or how. I breathed in and took one of the most difficult meetings I have ever had—not that it was long or loud. I went into his office, told him I would have to leave and take the project with me; he said why; I said I had heard rumors; he said of what; I didn't say, just added that things had to improve otherwise I would have to leave. He knew I knew, kept quiet for a long moment, then calmly said they will improve, I promise. The meeting took at most five minutes and I left. And things improved drastically in the coming weeks. The EIA team got re-energized; the quality of the submissions improved; and the technical discussions of details, often irrelevant, continued. We never talked about this again. Last Christmas, he sent me a picture of his family with all children and grandchildren, asking when I would come to Borneo again, as it had been more than 20 years.

We had a year of smooth operation of the EIA system. Still, I thought there were too many submissions, and there were too many submissions that did not make sense, which the planned EIA Compliance Survey confirmed. And so, despite the system in general being assessed a success, I asked the director to request the State Assembly for a change in the prescribed activities, a change that would result in fewer but more logical and rational applications. He agreed. This modification of the system was approved by the State Assembly just before the project and my assignment with the department ended.

Postevaluation

We had, for the EIA system, gone full circle: from technical system to professional skills development, to overload and tricky political issues, and finally to continued adjustments. I felt we had covered all the key aspects of organizational and individual professional capacity. Because the project design had laid the foundation, I think we all became better at juggling and dealing with TPPU issues. But what do I know?

Did we reach the professional capacity development objectives of the project? The planned outputs and activities were implemented, documented, and reached. The budget kept. As an external permanent in-house advisor, we reached impacts and results I could not have dreamt of. The cooperation and friendship with the director, the department's increased reputation, the activities undertaken in all six areas of the department, the networks created, and the exposure to new ways of doing things became for me a once-in-a-lifetime professional and personal journey. I know that Eric, Yabi, Tony, and the other professionals involved felt the same.

Did we increase the organizational and professional capacities of the department and its officers? I think so, but this I cannot document. Development of one's own and others' deep professional capacities is two completely different things. And development of an organization's and an individual's professional capacity is also two very different issues. I knew this, but never got a real handle of how to distinguish these aspects. And maybe it is not possible or necessary.

> *In 1927, Bohr expounded his principle that light is both wave-like and particle-like, simultaneously. The reality detected depends on the experimenter and his method. If you observe a photon with a particle detector, you get a particle. Observe the photon with a wave detector, and you get a wave. Neither, Bohr said, is more real or accurate. We can only see a wave or a particle at any one time, yet both descriptions are necessary to get a full sense of what light is. The two methods complement each other, and the simultaneous both/and becomes a better perspective than either/or.*[1]

To assess the capacity impact of my efforts on others is like asking a photon if it is a particle or a wave. I was both a particle and a wave. I was both submerged into the department and a wave passing through. I was for four years part of it all. We worked, we achieved outputs together, and we moved forward. What we learned, which capacities we improved, was our personal thing, not something that could be measured. If we had tried, we would have asked wrong questions, questions that would not have made us cleverer. But I can reflect on what I learned and which of my own professional capacities improved during my four years in Borneo.

I learned that the EIA system is nonsensical. This was the first time I realized that even if we do all we can, put in hours and energy, develop all the systems and procedures we think are needed, if the system is wrong, it all does not matter. I do not know what I would have done if I had known that the EIA system is such a wrong and inappropriate environmental tool, that it is mainly a tool for power and corruption, and that the environmental impact of the EIA system is microscopic. Unfortunately, we first really learn and improve our professional capacity when we are engulfed deeply in details and technicalities. In hindsight, the energy and hours wasted on a subsector or system that is useless or irrelevant are painful. Unfortunately, I had this painful experience again in the wastewater management, rural development, foreign aid, and alternative buildings technology sectors.

I learned that getting from A to B is in itself an achievement. The temptation to make implementation and the results we achieved look rational and straightforward is overwhelming, but in this large and complicated project, we got from A to B, we implemented all outputs and activities, and we reached what we had set out to do. To plan a four-year project and then implement it according to plan can, in hindsight, feel almost natural or obvious. But in four years, the project, and its results and impacts, could have gone in so many other directions. We could have had a new director, we could have had politicians that interfered too much, and we could have had officers not able to implement. It is only in hindsight we achieved what we achieved. The pleasure of creating and maintaining order in a complex process is why I like being a project manager: simple and complex at the same time.

I learned that all four implementation capacities are required to operate systems efficiently. I learned that to implement and operate a technical system effectively, even a bureaucratic and technocratic system as the EIA system, not one but four professional capacities were essential: the capacity to plan, rationalize, and structure activities and processes to manage the EIA system and get standardized outcomes; the capacity to maintain and develop human resources needed to administer the EIA system; the capacity to use, maintain, and expand influence and power to secure that the EIA system has sufficient acceptance and support from its key internal and external stakeholders; and the capacity to adjust and experiment for continuous development and survival of the EIA system to secure that the system does not lose its relevance. That the four different capacities were not only relevant, but necessary, surprised me. I experienced first-hand over the four years that, if the four different capacities were not present, the EIA system would fail. When rational capacities lacked, the system lacked objectivity, procedural straightforwardness, and efficiency. When people capacities lacked, the EIA system became unprofessionally managed. When political capacities lacked, the EIA system lost its legitimacy and became side-tracked. When experimental capabilities lacked, the system went bureaucratic, lost its ability to develop and respond to new demands and technologies, and lost its relevance within a surprisingly short time.

I learned that the different agendas of TPPU needed different levels of attention at different times during implementation. Not only were rational, people, power, and complex unforeseen capacities required to make the system efficient, but they required different amounts of attention at different times. I started to think of this as the *four-piston* attention mental model. Priority attention may first have to be given to system and technical skill development. Then two section heads start to quarrel and the conflict spreads to the full department—no way around giving this full attention. Then an environmental disaster happens on the other side of the island and the consequences, media, and politicians take center stage. I learned that I had to pay attention to all agendas, but, at different times, had to put much more energy and resources into an agenda that suddenly needed to be managed. The four agendas of TPPU moved up and down like pistons and there was no way around following their movement.

I learned that I forgot to include capacity levels and depth in the design. My project design included the four professional implementation capacities, the different agendas we must learn and juggle to become professional. All good. But I forgot to include and integrate the five-level depth in the design. I did not consider this was a new young department and, from there, build depth. When we began implementation of the EIA system, the department had very limited experience in managing submitted EIA reports, all theoretical with no experience and context. We got the new law enforced and we developed guidelines and internal manuals for how to deal with EIA submissions: level-one textbook stuff. Assessment of the reports was based on the assessment manual; all were approved, also because we had nothing to compare with. When we received more EIA reports, we became better at comparing reports within different environmental fields and between the different consultants submitting the reports. Assessment of these reports was now based on both the assessment manual and our comparison with earlier submitted reports. Still, we were reactive. We received and assessed. During the third year, we found it increasingly clear that we needed to be more proactive in dealing with the system. In the fourth year, we probably had moved to level two, getting closer to level three. All this just happened, with no conscious plan from my side. I should have thought through more carefully about how we should or could move up the professional experience ladder. This was a four-year project, so there would have been time.

I learned that overload and stress can be a good thing. EIA was only one area of the project. There were 5 other areas, 21 other outputs, and 54 other activities to be implemented. Twelve new outputs were added during implementation, a new law, and the publication of a coffee table photo book. There were 35 consultants, reporting to the embassy and home office; there were the professionals and staff in the department; there were working groups, external stakeholders, study tours, helicopter rides, site visits to the interior, dinners, and meetings. It was a whirlwind of agendas, people, activities, outputs, and deadlines. I had mainly planned with many outputs and activities to be sure that the project could connect to and benefit as many of the department professionals as possible. That succeeded. But I had also experienced in other projects that a too small agenda can result in side-lining and irrelevance of a project if priorities change. Better sometimes to set many ships in the sea, accept that some will sink, and hope others will float. The implementation of multiple activities and processes quickly and in parallel, the use of self-organizing teams, and the increased internal and external interactions and networking created overload and stress—and increased internal competition. Some professionals flourished and took the opportunity to excel and grow. Some withered. Some outputs had impacts beyond expectation and some folded. Some networks and friendships grew and deepened; some vanished. The overload and stress created turbulence, a whirlwind that shook all involved and resulted in new, unexpected results and unforeseen opportunities and directions.

I got better at dealing balanced with tricky backstage issues. Some will never perform, and I learned how to put them in a cool box, sideline them, so they did not get a chance to negatively impact the project. I got better at accepting that all people, everywhere, must survive. We all have a family to feed, a boss to please, and a job to keep, and our context determines how that can be done. I got to understand that the most important thing is that professionals always have one leg planted in their profession, in trying to do it right and professional, in creating impacts and improvements. The other leg may sometimes be planted in the reality of money and dependences, but only if both legs are planted there are we in trouble as we then forget to also be professionals, interested in our profession, in our field of competence, in making things better. I got better at knowing my own power platform, and when to use it to get us all back on track.

And I got to write my own little Heart of Darkness. *Tony told me we had reached the top. We were at the Heart of Borneo. At the top of the mountain range that surrounded the Maliau Basin. I had moved to Borneo three years ago, had visited villages, rivers, islands, forests, mountains, and had seen any rare tropical specie you can dream of. Yabi had served me bats and cobras. But I had never been to the heart of the Island, the Maliau Basin, the deepest and most difficult accessible mountain area at the end of the Kinabatangan River. One of the last frontiers where humans still were absent. Closed by the Government. This was off-limits. Unwelcomed territory.*

Tony Greer, my deputy, had lived in these deep forests for five years researching the 429 species in 125 genera and 14 tribes of the Bornean Geometridae of the subfamily Ennominae, or in other words, moths. He was the best environmental expert I have known. He was in the world's top five of experts that could recognise most bird species before he had seen them. For what use I never found out. He was British, understated, dry-humoured. After three days of driving, we reached the Maliau mountain range, left the 4WD behind and the two of us started the ascent, which would take three days. Up and down again. To say it was a hot day is to state the obvious, all days here are extremely hot and humid. We were at the equator.

And it was torture. Forget about a nice walk in the forest, forget about beautiful tropical animals, plants or flowers. This was deep ancient jungle. And that means full covered treetops with not a slice of sun coming through. And that means moist darkness. No colours, everything just grey and slippery. And not a sound. Not an animal or bird. Not fully true as after 100 m up the hillside, I got stung by a bee, or whatever it was, fell and slid back down the muddy hillside. There was no path, so we had to find our own way upwards through the dense vegetation. After five minutes all my clothes were soaked in sweat. Next came the leaches. Tony had been in the neighbourhood before and had told me to buy special leg covers that went above the knees. They did not do the trick. These leaches sit there on the floor, waiting and when you pass, they jump. And crawl under your clothes and down your legs into the boots. The first time I had to remove one from my leg I almost fainted. Blood running is not my thing. We camped the first night, not in a tent, too many leaches, but in a hanging bed Tony had attached between two trees. Did not sleep much that night. The next day went pretty much the same. Tough, unpleasant and torturous. We reached the summit in the late afternoon. How Tony knew this was the summit I still do not know. It all looked the same to me. Dense treetops and darkness. I had reached my Heart of Darkness. And I could see nothing.

There was no heart of darkness on Borneo. There was no Kurtz. There was only the Director Eric Juin, the politest professional I have met. A gentleman. He taught me that it is possible to face problems with dignity and that we have no choice but to balance the impossible demands life puts on our shoulders. And he taught me to not like but at least appreciate Nasi Goreng. And there was Tony, the moth expert, Yabi, the knower of all things edible, and there was the State Champion. After our Maliau expedition, I was back on the badminton court getting hammered by the kids. I did not know the name of the State champion or his teammates, they did not speak English and I did not speak Malay, but for some reason had they decided it was fine to use six hours every week for three years to give me a beating. That was heart and it was light. I was happy.

TPPU1: Use Projects to Accumulate Deep TPPU Reference Points

Only some of our professional reference points and experiences give us professional TPPU depth. I find it useful to think of the professional experience-based reference points that give us depth as *dense* reference points, as experiences where we have experienced and been part of a *full professional process from planning, implementation, to evaluation.* Such dense experiences become a deep experience-based and evaluated reference point in our internal library. We can label these dense reference points *projects*, as projects are defined by plan, implementation, and evaluation (PIE), and if we have managed a process, or project, with a full

PIE cycle, this will unavoidably provide us with a dense, deep professional experience or reference point. And as each of these dense reference points in our internal memory library has a unique context, we should think of the unique context for each PIE reference point as the four contexts of TPPU, or a TPPU context. We get better at what we do when we accumulate *deep* knowledge from having been engulfed in a professional PIE reference point long enough to understand its contextual TPPU complexities. This gives our neural spreading activation system strong, dense, and deep reference points to work with.

Professional PIE reference point	Professional reference point with TPPC contexts—**depth**	Professional reference point referenced—**width**

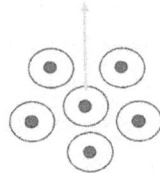

Reference point	Reference point with context	Reference point referenced

Units for professionalism

To become a professional project manager, the issue of professional depth is critical. Without such deep reference points, professionally, we will not be taken seriously. This is the deep experiences that other professionals assess and judge us upon. Most professional statements or project stories have some depth. We get the depth when we understand the meaning of what is being told or written, what is below and behind. What we, and our peers, therefore always want is a way to distinguish between the deep and the shallow: Does it have depth? Most professional interactions are about that question: Is this bluff or for real? Does the result stem from deep contextual experience or is it just an estimate from shallow experiences?[2] Professional capacity has much to do with the ability to distinguish between shallow and deep experiences. Both our own and others.

Only through gaining deep professional expertise in a specific topic, any professional topic, do we recognize its depth and complexity. For the topics we have attained depth, we immediately know when others talk nonsense, and we can use this experience of depth to also calibrate our own built-in illusion of explanatory depth,[3] the illusion that makes us think we understand most things with far greater detail, coherence, and depth than we really do. This extends to how we think about and use mental models for globalization, economic markets, organizations, professionalism, TPPU contexts, and virtually any complex professional issue we can (mis)understand. As during our career we only attain real depth for a few professional issues, issues where we really know what we are talking about, we must for all the other issues and areas develop and use mental models, abstractions, and simplified thought patterns to streamline reality down to something we can get our minds around. We must supplement depth with reference points and mental models obtained from variation and exposure, from what others have experienced or documented, from having been involved in many projects, in many different contexts, sectors, and locations.

TPPU2: Juggle the Four Implementation Agendas

One of the first things I learned after I left university and entered the working professionals was that it was not only outputs but also processes and people that mattered to create good results, and that results depend on intricate implementation processes. In the 1990s, I worked for three years in the health care sector in Denmark and one conversation still stands clear. The conversation took place just a couple of weeks after we had finished three books on how hospitals could become more professionally managed. The books were about quality assurance systems, and the main point was that professional quality could be improved and guaranteed through better continuity between doctors and patients and implementation of team-based systematic quality monitoring.

The chief doctor, whom I had written the books with, 20 years my senior, had invited me to his house for dinner and we got into a discussion of what we thought were the best results of our efforts. The chief doctor did, to my big surprise, think that the most important result was something that I in fact only had paid little attention to. He found that it was the process that had had the biggest impact on the quality of work in the department. The fact that the project had been implemented through interdisciplinary teams had meant that we had forced increased cooperation not only between the 150 doctors and nurses, but also with the more than 30 internal and external different professional disciplines that had been involved. This had meant that interprofessional understandings and cooperation had greatly improved. Different professional groups now knew each other better and had a better understanding and respect for their different professional fields. This, he found, was the main reason for the improved quality of the professional decisions and patient treatment we had documented and proven. The reason was not our rather sophisticated quality assurance systems, but the improved personal friendships, networks, and exchange of knowledge. He even went as far as to say that he was not sure if they would continue to implement the quality assurance system, as he found the organizational and technological developments in the health care sector moved too fast for any rigid system-based management system.

As a young ambitious organizational management consultant, I had mainly seen the process as a means to an end; the end being to innovate, invent, develop, and implement a system that could improve and guarantee the professional quality of hospital work, not only in this department in this hospital, but in the country. I admit I found it difficult to accept his assessment. That the process was the result, and the result, the technical rational system we had developed and implemented through great care and efforts, was of less importance than how we had done what during the years was hard to swallow. This was a system which I had worked with them almost nonstop for three years, which had resulted in three books, which is still being reprinted today, which had been reported in all national newspapers, which the Minister of Health had presented in the evening news on TV, and which we had toured the country with. And now he said he was not sure he would continue the system!

This was the first time I had to seriously reconsider the relation between results and processes and the impact of emergence through multiple task forces operating simultaneously, creating system overload and a bit of uncontrollable chaos. My rational mental model had come under attack. The doctor had confronted me with other equally important rationalities and my professional world certainly had become more complex. When did I, to a higher degree, accept the importance of processes, networks, and emergence? Certainly not when I was on Dreyfus and Dreyfus' capacity level one or two, where results, ambitions, and achievements had a clear and all-consuming focus. I wanted to get there, and I wanted to get there fast.

I have realized that it is only on the first levels we can focus almost exclusively on the technical issues, as this is where we start to develop the professional technical skills of our profession that will take us through our career. Some stay technical nerds throughout, but they are few and far between (and often not so successful). For all the rest of us, when we get closer to level three, we will be asked to or request to manage something, to be responsible for implementation of an assignment, get things from A to B, manage people, plan, and execute. And then we need to add to the technical skills, the three other implementation skills of cooperation, power, and emergence.

The technical skills required by our profession are always the starting point, our professional foundation. Throughout, we must be **technically** competent and experienced with respect to the technical substance, and we must be familiar with a range of planning, scheduling, budgeting, control, and monitoring techniques. We must be able to rationally analyze, propose, implement, and evaluate technical problems and solutions, and we must be able to control the process through the basic project management issues of budget control, accounting, scheduling, timing and phasing, assigning responsibilities, keeping deadlines, progress reporting, and monitoring. The phased project cycle approach is a rational implementation tool I have used in all my projects, and that, if used properly, increases effectiveness as it makes implementation unfold in a logically sequenced manner. The technical platform performs the core process around which the three other types of implementation processes revolve (people, power, and the complex unforeseen). Not only because technical rationality increases effectiveness, but, in my experience, also because if implementation is not seen as rational, we will lose impact and credibility because implementation of rational processes legitimates, we must use accepted rational approaches and processes to get legitimacy, recognition, and acceptance. The rational techniques contribute to an appearance of professionalism, competence, and logic in implementation. In fact, if we do not implement with technical rationality, time and energy will be wasted on unnecessary questions, suspicions, accounting, progress reporting, and communication with confused stakeholders.

All professional achievements are achieved in **cooperation** with other professionals, and any implementation process therefore requires competence in communication and consultation, team building, facilitation, and involvement and development of the professionals around us. I have always found the deliberate use of teams to plan, implement, and evaluate outputs and activities, on creating challenges which are met and overcome collectively, a good and safe starting point to create involvement and commitment. But, of course, we must also use more subtle ways, energy, charm, or enthusiasm, to get participation or commitment for specific issues from specific people. The most difficult issue, in my experience, has been to achieve true participation and involvement throughout the full project cycle, from design, financial allocation, selection of participants, to active involvement in implementation, progress monitoring, completion, and impact evaluation. I know from myself that it is only then that deep professional learning happens. In real life, however, full project cycle participation is difficult to attain. Participation is often only linked to involvement in implementation of activities, while others deal with planning, budget control, monitoring, and evaluation, or participation is pushed in the background as focus is retained on rational issues of control and content, technology, procedures, budgets, and deadlines. When the optimal is not possible, the least I can do is to be honest and clearly announce the degree of participation that can be expected in the different phases of the project cycle. Better than nothing and for sure better than the fake participation processes that often play out.

Anyone who has managed or been involved in a project or process knows that implementation involves serious processes of **power**, special interests, conflicts, influence, struggle for resources, positioning, coalitions, negotiations, deals, arguments, and manipulation. And they know that to achieve goals we, apart from technical and participatory skills, also need to be able to use influence and power. For such subtle and complex issues, no predefined processes or blueprints exist, and political implementation capacities are seldom described in textbooks. They can seem illegitimate, but political processes are real, essential, and unavoidable and the capacities required, when used with flair and sensitivity, are effective tools to improve outputs and impacts. We need to be able to get action from a manager who has given agreement but does nothing in practice, to get those who are making unreasonable demands to back off, tactfully, to avoid or deal appropriately with competing activities that delay progress, or to deal with budget and money issues that have a direct impact on activities and outputs. In my experience, the two key issues we must be able to deal with are to have knowledge of the power structures and then to position ourselves within these power structures. We need to understand the political playing field: Who is in power, who likes who, and who really takes decisions. We need to have a sensitivity to the power and influence of key individuals and groups. And for that, we need to continuously acquire knowledge and information to understand the internal and external power agendas. We need to get and use internal and external informants to receive valuable political information on the different power or conflict issues. And then we need to position ourselves, our effort, or project within this playing field. This requires a capacity for positioning within the established power structure to improve aims, results, and impact. Implementation always happens concurrently with numerous other agendas, which create competition for attention and resources. The positioning processes require continuous attempts at getting in positions that make it possible to influence favorable implementation, to negotiate, to legitimize and to promote plans and ideas. We need to get into positions where we can negotiate and sell plans and ideas, change or manipulate perceptions, and legitimize proposals and results. We need to be in a position where we can overcome resistance.

With experience, we know better what to expect during implementation, and we know that we will encounter not only technical, people, and power issues but also *complex* unforeseen issues, opportunities, and problems. And we know that we must have the ability to deal with these emergent issues. We know that change happens not only because of our deliberate plans and implementation efforts, but also because of unanticipated financial shifts, crises, mismanagement, accidents, coincidences, and fortuitous events. We know that momentum can emerge out of random events and that small events can have huge effects (and huge efforts negligible effects). We know that situations can become messy; that we must tolerate ambiguity, be pragmatic and opportunistic, and respond flexibly to events as they unfold, and continuously adapt; and that we, at times, will have to muddle through with purpose. On recollection, I have used emergence when I have slipstreamed to something opportune passing by, when I consciously have overloaded the system through implementation of multiple processes simultaneously to set people and the organization under stress, and when I have increased internal and external interactions and networking to increase complexity and decrease process and impact control to create unexpected new insights and ways of doing things.

To become professional implementors, we need structure and technical knowledge, we need other people to support us, we need power on our side, and we need to be pragmatically adaptable and creative. These four skills correspond to our four professional contexts and implementation agendas. As a mental model, they have helped me to better and quickly understand what is required and how to be a good efficient project manager, to analyze an organization, to design a project, to make a plan or strategy, or to understand why an attempt failed. It is my experience that it is only by being competent in juggling all four different professional agendas that we become truly professionals, and that in implementation, it is key to be able to switch attention between the four agendas and be able to quickly shift focus from rational planning issues to people issues, to political issues, or to emerging issues. Our ability to get from A to B improves with our ability to continuously juggle and prioritize between these four different implementation agendas. In complex settings, we cannot rely on or become successful by only being good on one of the professional implementation agendas. That is not how professional work works.

TPPU3: Make Plans

I have found it beneficial to define and think of my professional experiences as stand-alone projects. This project angle makes it easier not only to keep track of my experiences (my job is not a job, but a string of projects), but also to become better at evaluating my own plans and expectation for each project. A project has a start and end point and is a time-constrained clearly defined effort to get from A to B through the implementation of a preconceived plan. The plan is the combination of methods and techniques that are applied to get us from A to B. The plan is described with chains and processes of actions, activities, and outputs. Because it has a start and end point, we think through and plan the process required to achieve the outputs and, consciously or unconsciously, evaluate the process and outputs after the job is done. This plan, implement, and evaluate process is key to how we accumulate professional experience.

Looking back, I can see that my plans for the 225 projects I have been involved in have gone from simple and slightly dumb to overly deliberate and complicated and back to simple but less dumb. And I have come to better acknowledge that if our professional capacities, for example, are at level one, the plan will be level one student stuff; if we get the context wrong, the plan is useless; and if we do not have the knowledge or ability to implement a plan in relation to technical, people, political and complex process issues, the plan will go nowhere.

The key elements in making a plan are simple: Select the objectives, outputs, and processes of activities and determine the required inputs (the LFA to planning). For each objective, there is a pool of possible outputs, and likewise, for each output, there is a pool of different possible processes of activities and inputs that can be planned, allocated, and implemented to reach the output. However, to get the plan right requires that we initially thoroughly think through and include somewhere in the plan the *distinctions between technical, people, political, and complex contexts* as these provide the platform for a good plan.

When my plans have worked, they have *focused on action* and linked to on-going, day-to-day processes, problems, and interests. We need to get as quickly as possible to action and action learning. Plans must therefore also be *concrete, specific, and realistic*. If it is not possible within few minutes to describe the key aims, outputs, and methods of the plan, or if the plan shows unrealistic links between outputs and inputs, something is likely wrong. In my experience, it is always best to work the LFA bottom up, start with the actual inputs in money or time allocated, and then move up through the planning of activities within that budget, which then will lead us to realistic or potential achievable outputs and objectives. Unfortunately, most plans are written top town beginning with overambitious objectives and assumptions compared to actual available inputs. Balanced ambitions and modesty usually make the most convincing plans. And then they, of course, have to be *context specific*. We shall draw on our previous experience, best practices, and projects to illustrate what might be possible, but this then must be combined with a recognition of what is unique and specific for this specific plan.

After conceptualization, plans are *written down*, but, unfortunately, as with putting down our deep professional project stories to paper, the issue of writing it down is not straightforward. We can increase the acceptability of the plan by using positive result-oriented language such as develop, improve, grow, maintain, and do—words that imply action and progress; words that give the impression that the problem already has been well understood and that positive steps can be taken to make things progress and develop in the desired direction. This also means there are many words we cannot use. We decrease the acceptability of a plan by using words and language that imply procrastination or delayed action as more homework must be done. And we decrease acceptability by using negative formulations or by putting to paper something that should have been kept backstage and therefore creates resistance or noncommitment. This includes undertaking contextual problem tree, stakeholder, SWOT (strengths, weaknesses, opportunities, and threats), resource dependency, or any other context analyses. *Include* these in our written plan. As there is no such thing as a factual description of complex structures or problems, context analysis will always be partial and therefore also partly wrong. The analysis of complex issues, written down, will always be wrong about many aspects, oversimplistic, and therefore, for many stakeholders, insulting or amateurish.

As professionals, whether we like it or not, we will never get away from planning and the need to continuously improve our ability to make and write down a plan. Predicting and making a plan for the future is our professional life blood, as it is for all living organisms, all the way down to the tiniest cells.

TPPU4: Expand Your Professional Network

My professional friends and colleagues anchor and surround me wherever I am. Put me anywhere in the world and I will surround myself with similar-minded professionals. I will never feel alone, de-anchored. There are more than three billion of us. Having worked for many years as a professional has meant that my network of professionals has become big, which is good as professional survival and development is also a number game; we will not make it with a network of five professionals. My LinkedIn network has passed 10,000. Having been involved in projects worldwide has given me a *global* network of professionals I have worked with and can rely on. I have, in average, from each project, continued to have professional contact with three professionals, which today has given me a valuable global network of around 600 professionals. And then I have my local network, the network I am working in now. After more than a decade in South Africa, my current *local* professional network is around 800 professionals, professionals I have worked with or helped and can call upon for advice, cooperation, and further networking. This network is especially important as an entrepreneur as I constantly chase projects, contracts, and professionals to join as independent specialized team members.

And finally, I have my *tight* network of professionals, the professionals that daily surround me. Having a tight network of good professionals, being with people I like and respect, and doing things I like to do in complex processes that I find ambitious and challenging, make me most productive, and happy. Earlier in my career, my work brought me into situations where I had to deal and compete with professionals I did not like. Normally, the ignore strategy worked, but not always; sometimes they came too close. Work places, decisions of bosses, and projects bind us to professionals we spend most time with. And they might not be the ones we want to spend time with. My professional interests have sometimes led me to develop and choose projects and then these have led to the people that surround me, whether I liked them or not. The project chose, not me. My agro-development projects in South Africa for several years took me offtrack in relation to the people and professionals I wanted to be surrounded by. Today, if I take a normal month, I will not have spent any time with professionals I do not like or not think are interesting to work with. It has taken me time to become selective and spoilt with who surrounds me. I believe in the saying that we are the average of our five best friends. This also counts for the professionals we spend most time with. And this is why I have become better at taking a honest look around and assess if I am happy and good with being the average of the five professionals that surround me and that I spend most time with.

So who are the professionals in my global and local networks? I went through the numbers, looked at my list of local and global professionals, and looked for patterns. I found five.

They are professionals not because they say they are or because they have a paper to prove they are. They are professionals when I think they are. Being a professional is not a label we can give ourselves. It is a description we can hope others apply to us. To belong to a profession means to have the capacity to undertake specialized and skilled work within this profession. And professionals can only continue to be called professional within a profession if they continuously upgrade existing professional skills and learn new skills through re-education. Being a professional is not a thing achieved and kept. Being a professional is not something we are forever; we are only a professional if it is continuously confirmed by our peers. I am a critical peer.

They are professionals that have specialized professional skills I do not have. Historically, when we became more and more specialized, we began to profess our skill to others and vowed to perform our trade to the best known standard.[4] With a reputation to uphold, trusted workers who had specific tasks to do were considered professionals. Early on, we only recognized three professions: divinity, medicine, and law, the so-called learned professions. Later came dentistry, civil engineering, logistics, architecture, and accounting. With the rise of technology and occupational specialization, many other fields started to claim professional status: mechanical engineering, pharmacy, veterinary medicine, psychology, nursing, teaching, librarianship, optometry, architecture, social work, and even project management with professional project managers like me that need other professions on board to create good professional results and achievements.

They do not talk nonsense. A professional is a scientist in the sense that a professional observes data, analyzes, thinks, does the best to explain phenomena, and acts accordingly. This means that a professional must be grounded in science and scientific thinking and must be an empiricist that, continuously, throughout the professional career experiments, assesses, acts, evaluates, revises, and improves. There are no nonsense speakers in my network.

They are not amateurs, dilettantes, or charlatans. A professional makes a living in his or her profession. A professional derives income from specific and specialized knowledge. And the professionals pursue that profession openly, that is, engineers declare themselves to be engineers, chemists themselves to be chemists, and so on. The opposite of a professional is an amateur, one who engages in an activity for love rather than money, or a dilettante, one who lacks the seriousness of those who must live by such work. Those who declare membership in a profession to which they do not belong are mere charlatans, quacks, or impostors. In contexts where almost all are professionals, it is difficult to get away with posturing and dilettantism as there are too many peers, whereas in contexts where few are professionals, it is easier and more charlatans and chancers appear. I have met several of those, and unfortunately, as they are also charming and clever, it can take time to realize they are charlatans and not professionals.

They are polite, trustful, and cooperative. To be a professional always requires collaboration and sharing. A professional knows the importance of exchange, trust, dialogue, interaction, connection, borrowing, and blending, and knows that disagreement, hostility, and conflict are counterproductive. Professionalism is so much more than each of us being clever all by ourselves. Professionalism is a team sport. The professionals on my list are good and polite people; they are professionals I like, respect, and trust.

I have been involved in hundreds of projects and met thousands of professionals and my professional network has grown over time. It has grown every time other professionals have built *trust in me*, and I have learned to trust my experiences and the professionals I met. It is a rarity to be cheated, so I have learned not to expect it. And that helps. It means I unconditionally share information, reports, documents, proposals, and concepts, and every time I have given or shared something not expected, my network has expanded. It has grown when I have made them shine.

Growing our professional network has a lot to do with *giving* first—giving without expecting returns. A Buddhist monk opened my eyes to the art of giving. At the end of my university years, I studied at Bangkok's Chulalongkorn University and at one of our after-study sit-downs with the drivers in the backroom, sharing Mekong whiskey and time, a monk joined and the discussion turned to the many beggars on the street and the stories of the beggars being in syndicates and exploited. I asked him if he thought I should give them something. I still remember his answer 40 years later. He said that I should give when it felt right as we never can control the steps following any act of giving. If I began to think about how the money would be used, the act of giving will go astray. Giving has to come with heart and trust. I have experienced that the monk was right.

TPPU5: Deal With Power Games

Our professional life is an unending stream of small power struggles and challenges. Sometimes, our boss is impossible, and the days are miserable. Sometimes, a little bureaucrat is holding back payment of our invoice, and we must find ways to deal with him. Sometimes, a colleague openly resists our idea, thereby challenging our position, and we must find ways to overcome her resistance and safeguard our position. Our career is filled with these small power struggles and the ups and downs they bring. These are the power struggles we, in good periods, win without really noticing. We win most of them based on the place we have in the positional hierarchy and our social capital. They are the daily small power struggles we need to win to become successful and have impact. With time, I have become more conscious of the place I have in the hierarchy that surrounds me and to use this place to win or pull back. When I win these power games, large or small, the win seldom takes much attention. I just move on to the next small power struggle that needs to be won. What I remember, of course, are the times I have lost and been hurt. These are painful and therefore easy to retrieve a memory of.

I went through my jobs and projects to find the occasions and persons that had made me lose. It came to five occasions and five persons: five times where I have been on the wrong side of power struggles, five times I have been challenged and hurt. These painful clashes proved to be rare incidents. And as two of these happened in the last decade, I have also experienced that I have not been able to keep them out of my life. Five lost power stories, five different contexts, spanning four decades, any lessons to be learned? Two stories concerned people trying to position themselves better in the organizational hierarchy by trying to get me out of the way, three stories concerned people playing, for me, unknown games to safeguard, enrich, or position themselves better. The games were mostly played indirectly and involved strategies to damage my reputation. The more often I see and recognize patterns, the better I get at dealing with them. But because these blows have happened seldom, it is difficult to talk of patterns. They feel punctuated and random. And if there is no pattern to recognize, there is little learning to be had. My responses have varied from running, ducking, or failed counterattacks. Not really anything to learn there either. So I just have to lean back and wait for the next blow to strike me. And I am fine with that because maybe the real lesson learned from these power clashes is not that I should become better at fighting back, but the very fact that they are so rare, over a full length of a career, means that they are outliers and that what we should prepare ourselves for all the normal professionals and situations where trust, fairness, and cooperation are the names of the game.

My memorable power struggles have been rare outliers and because of this, I have placed The Podium, The Copy Machine, The Ambassador, The Charlatans, and The Wicked One power stories on my homepage.[5] You are welcome to take a look; they are depressingly entertaining.

TPPU6: Use Numbers and Logic, Think in Levels and Recognize Patterns

Use Numbers and Logic

Context complexity makes professional life interesting, but complex contexts are also hard to get hold of. Of course, if they were not hard to grasp, they would not be complex. The use of numbers and logic has sometimes helped me cope better with these complexities. Numbers and logics bring the level of complexity down a notch. Counting, number sense, order of magnitude, the Pareto principle, exponentiality, and regression to the mean have helped me to at least deal a little better with complexity and emergence in my professional world.

If we are not able to do arithmetic, we are doomed to talk nonsense. In many cases, all we need to avoid nonsense is the simplest form of arithmetic, counting.[6] Probability is nothing but common sense reduced to calculation, and the basis of probability theory is counting. This is a powerful tool. When faced with a complex issue, we can resolve the question not by examining our political predispositions or arguing for whatever agrees with these, but by examining the evidence, counting the number of favorable cases, and comparing it with the number of those that are not. Add to this *number sense*, the ability of having fluidity and flexibility with numbers, a sense of what numbers mean, and an ability to use numbers to negotiate the world and make comparisons.[7] The lack of number sense is a big professional disqualifier. Then add *order-of-magnitude* estimates.[8] How many pianos are repaired in Johannesburg each year? Answering this requires making reasonable guesses about such things as the fraction of people having pianos and how long it takes to repair them. Anyone can do that. No background in advanced mathematics is required, just the self-confidence to take on the problem. Observation, simplified assumptions, and simple calculations can get us close to the truth, which is not solely the province of mathematicians or engineers but a province for all professionals.

Add the *Pareto principle* to this arsenal of logical tools to improve our ability to deal with complexity.[9] Figures like "the top 1 percent of the population controls 35 percent of all wealth" is normally reported as shocking, as if the normal order of things has been disrupted, as if the appearance of anything other than a linear distribution of money or messages or effort was a surprise of the highest order. It is not. And should not be. The 80/20 Pareto rule often provides the standard and normal distribution: The richest or busiest or most connected professionals in a system will account for much, much more wealth or activity or connectedness than the average. Pareto called this pattern the predictable imbalance and we are failing to predict it, even though it is everywhere. Part of our failure to expect the expected is that we have been taught that the paradigmatic distribution of large systems is the Gaussian bell-curve distribution. In a bell-curve distribution, like height, the average and the median (the middle point in the system) are the same. Pareto distributions are nothing like that: The 80/20 weighting means that the average is far from the middle. This, in turn, means that in such systems, most professionals (or whatever is being measured) are below average, a pattern encapsulated in the joke: *Bill Gates walks into a bar and makes everybody a billionaire, on average.* The Pareto distribution shows up in a remarkably wide array of complex systems. The magnitude of earthquakes, the popularity of books, and the social connectedness of professionals. Until we know which systems are Pareto distributions, and will remain so even after any intervention, we have not even started thinking about them in the right way. There is very little common sense or intuition in the Pareto principle. The Pareto principle shows us why we need to study to become professional.

And then again add to all this an understanding of *exponentiality.*[10] Exponential sequences are where things begin small, very small, but once they start growing, they grow faster and faster. To understand exponentiality and its ramifications is an ever more important professional capacity. After 1990, we entered the second globalization and here, some of the dramatic accelerations can elude our grasp: accelerations in science and technology, smartphones and language translation, big data analytics, self-driving vehicles, AI, robotics, solar cells, biotech, genomics, and neuroscience. While these fields may be growing very fast on their own, the combinatorial effect, the accelerating influence each has on the others, is dramatic and at times exponential. We are not evolutionarily geared for exponentiality. Almost every structure and method we have developed to manage our societies, governments, democracy, education, and health care systems is designed to function in a predictable, linear world, where spikes or downturns are seen as crises. Thus, it is unsurprising that the exponential pace of change in many areas is causing political, social, and psychological disquiet and stress. When Albert Einstein was asked what the greatest force in the world was, he replied without hesitation: compound interest. But we also must be careful not overdoing exponentiality, as luckily we also live under the law of *regression to the mean,*[11] a term from statistics that in real life means anomalies are anomalies and coincidences happen, all the time and with stunning frequency. The main thing regression to the mean tells us is that the next thing to happen is very likely to be normal, boring, ordinary, and predictable. Regression to the mean teaches us not to be so excitable and not so worried: Life really will, for the most part, be boring and predictable. Heeding the law of regression to the mean helps us calm down, pay attention to the long term and big picture, and react with more patience to crises large and small.

Think in Levels

I have come to realize that another key to cope with complexity is to practice again and again the capacity to understand levels. Literature, fiction, and movies have, for me, provided a platform to practice the understanding of different levels of complexity. When I have just finished a book, say Albert S. Pinol's brilliant *Pandora in the Congo*,[12] ask me what it was about. And I struggle big time. I would start out with telling parts of the story line, but then quickly insert passages on what I think the author wanted to tell us, and from there onward, it becomes a confusing mix and match of story, intentions, and meanings. I am likely not alone in this. To provide orally a coherent summary of complex works is not an easy task or skill. And normally, I stay away from it—but not in my head. I have found it a useful intellectual exercise to think of any book or movie I have just read or seen through a layered mental model of story line, persons, power, and big picture context.

The first layer is the story as it is, the actual story line, what happened to who and when. The key is to always start with this first layer, rationally and objectively tell it as it is. Normally if this is not possible, then, likely, it was a bad movie or book. The storyline did not come through. Then I move on to one, but only one, of the other layers to understand a book or movie, and what the author or film director meant to tell us. One layer is to try to understand and explain the book or movie on the individual level: What did we get to know and learn from the main persons, their feelings, problems, ambitions, angst, and alienation? What did it tell me of our existential condition? Another layer would be to try to understand the book or movie on the power level: What did we get to know and learn from the interactions between groups, their power struggle, political agendas, and games? Yet another layer would be to understand the book or movie at the big picture societal levels: What did we get to know and learn about our society, the economy, and how the system works.

All good movies, books, or stories have the potential to be understood, explained, or analyzed on different layers. This is also why we normally stumble when we are asked the simple question: What was the book about? My advice would be: When people ask, tell the story line as it is in a minute; then if time and energy allow and the listener is responsive, go to one of the other layers, but be clear about which one you choose. If we have sufficient time, attention, and concentration, it might be possible to discuss or try to understand all layers of potential meanings. Movies and books are good platforms for experimenting, testing, and challenging our capacity to understand complex contexts. Books of fiction and nonfiction, reading in general, are, apart from our own slowly accumulated one-by-one experiences, an excellent entry to get new reference points and knowledge of complex issues.

One of the books that first pointed to me, and many others with me, the importance of different layers of understanding was Joseph Conrad's *Heart of Darkness*.[13] Conrad's famous book is based on a real journey the author took to the Congo in 1890 during King Leopold's horrific rule. It is Marlow's fantastic, imaginative journey to find a man named Kurtz who has lost his mind in the African jungle. It is a journey into our inner space, a metaphorical investigation into the turbid waters of the human soul. It is a political journey into the dark heart of European colonialism. It is a nightmare journey into horror. It is a journey to nowhere, set on a boat lying motionless and at anchor on the River Thames, which also "has been one of the dark places on the earth."[14] There is no shortage of journeys to talk and think about in relation to *Heart of Darkness*. Few books have had such a profound effect on me as my passage toward understanding this little book. The first time I read the book, I was 19 and pretty much took *Heart of Darkness* at face value. I read and understood the story line of the book as it was. I read a densely written, uncomfortable, claustrophobic, and strange kind of adventure story. I was immensely fascinated, but I did not quite understand the story or the vague, difficult, ponderously adjectival English.

I have since re-read *Heart of Darkness* many times, and I began to see more clearly the book at many different levels—how beautifully Conrad brings out their meanings—and I felt even more awed by Conrad and his little book. I came to understand something of those other journeys in the book. I started to see how some writers can say one thing but mean multiple others. Marlow's boat was steaming into the soul of the man and that was the real heart of darkness. Or, at least, it might be. Nothing in the book was definite, and this very complexity and uncertainty also overwhelmed me. There were no easy answers. I began to feel the fascination and intoxication of complexity. I learned from *Heart of Darkness* a new way to read—a new way that included layers of understanding and different starting points for understanding books, movies, and our private and professional contexts.

I started to see and understand the book from the individual human condition point of view. *Heart of Darkness* is the story of a journey within. Marlow's journey and Kurtz's journey to Congo is a journey to the Congo of our mind. By narrating the outer journey to Congo, Conrad indirectly tells the inner journey. As the outer Congo is full of fear, terror, savagery, and forces of temptation, so is our inner Congo full of such dark forces. To fully understand our inner Congo, it is necessary to make outer Congo journeys, to engage in and experience real-life complex situations. Kurtz, during his journey, descended into the subconscious of dark forces and failed to handle these forces and be able to return from them. Marlow, on the other hand, descended with awareness and a sense of self-restraint and unflinching and unwavering loyalty to human standards and norms. He made the inner journey cautiously and returned.

I came to appreciate that the book, of course, also tells an outward journey story: the brave uncovering by Conrad of the negative impacts of European colonialism and imperialism for resource exploitation hidden in the slogans of spreading civilization at that time. I saw and understood the book from the power and societal point of view. The novel describes the ravages of imperialism during its journey to the heart of Africa. The very last line of the book sees the Thames, not the Congo, lead "into the heart of an immense darkness."

And it is here that I hit the final realization on my journey of discovery with Conrad. *Heart of Darkness* is so difficult and ambiguous that I realized I cannot fully resolve its challenges. And the way it is written, nor will anyone else. We cannot always find final solutions and answers. And we can both love a book and find it troubling. The road does not always have an end. The journey continues, even for a small book that is more than 100 years old. I have come increasingly to appreciate *Heart of Darkness* from *the complex emergent point of view,* the point where ambiguity and complexity rule.

As well as being an extraordinary story, *Heart of Darkness* contains some of the most beautiful use of language in English literature (from a person born in Poland, became a seaman at 16, and spent most of his time in France and South America before he, in his 30s, wrote this book in English, his third language). *Heart of Darkness* is written almost as an extended symbolic poem affecting all who read it with the breath of ideas and the beauty of its words. One of the most fascinating elements of Conrad's work lies in his insistence on the inherent inability of words to express the real world, in all of its beautiful or horrific truth. Marlow's journey is full of encounters with things that are unspeakable, with words that are uninterpretable, and with a world that is eminently inscrutable. In this way, language fails time and time again to do what it is meant to do: to describe and communicate. It is summed up when Marlow tells his audience that "it is impossible to convey the life-sensation of any given epoch of one's existence, that which makes its truth, its meaning, its subtle and penetrating essence. We live, as we dream, alone."

There are different ways to understand complex issues and contexts, methods we can practice and get better at either by doing or by reading and thinking, but sometimes it is equally important and useful just to accept ambiguity and complexity. Sometimes, some things are so complex and complicated that they are outside our field of experience and reference points. This does not mean we should stop thinking about them, even when we know they have no real solution or end point. I now know that something always settles and that I should not get too frustrated in not understanding it all. When we have experienced or read something similar multiple times, it starts to gets easier because the reference points are accumulating somewhere in our brain. And that is why some books, fiction or nonfiction, are a pleasure to re-read, *Heart of Darkness* to mention one.

Recognize Short Process Patterns

Patterns are everywhere and they take many forms: short term, long term, fluctuated, punctuated, repeatable, nonrepeatable, and overlapping.

Pattern recognition is a key ingredient in accumulated professional experience and intelligence. Recognizing patterns of complex contexts is what we get better at. Memory is the process of recognizing that a pattern of neural activation that is occurring now is similar to a pattern that occurred before. Our mind blends and completes complex patterns so that we can react adaptively and predict more correctly. Through my involvement in many different projects and contexts, I have slowly become better at recognizing how professional patterns materialize and unfold.

We often panic when we feel the professional process we are in is chaotic and out of control. But panic is not always the best way to react. In fact, we must actively pursue chaos and open-endedness, not always but sometimes. I taught group dynamics in 1991 at the Copenhagen Educational Centre. The half-year course was structured around a series of group interaction exercises to show different aspects of group dynamics. I still remember the impact the social stratification exercises had on all, how we very quickly assess, label, and rank each other in relation to intelligence, influence, or capacity, even in a group that has just been established, and how hardwired and difficult it is to change this mechanism. And how this stratification normally gets it right. And I remember the exercises and lessons that showed that processes are most effective when they use dynamic patterns of systematic switching between zooming in and out to come from A to B. A group has the task to develop a strategy. The best process to get this strategy as good as possible requires to shift between processes of opening up and broadening our views, possibilities, and options, followed by processes of narrowing and focusing these into a decision. And this must happen several times in the process of trying to get from A to B. Open up to see a range of objectives, focus to select the most appropriate, then again open up to see different ways to get to the objectives, before zooming in to select the methods and activities that would work best, and so on. This zooming in and out method stuck in my memory, and I have found it very useful. It has made me better at process management. It has made me calmer. I know when the process should become and feel a bit chaotic, and I know when we must focus and take decisions to move forward. Any good process from A to B will have patterns of zooming in and out, of chaos and control, and we have to be comfortable with these patterns. Complications and complexity is all around us, and we often want to take control and create small pockets of stability and predictability. The zooming in and out mental model helped me to understand that these pockets of control are fine but they are also comfort zones, which we sometimes should resist and not stay in for too long. The importance of letting go at specific times during a process took me time to get under my professional rational skin. To be honest, I am still not fully there. I still place too much importance on control, results, and outputs, but I am getting better at knowing when we need to zoom out and let go. Even privately. The first two weeks of my holiday is always the same. I make elaborate plans to create stability and predictability even here on a holiday: where to sleep and eat, what to see. Then after the first week, calm, flexibility, and carelessness slowly take over. The longer the holiday goes on, I realize that my attempt to create stability and predictability is a bit counterproductive and the better I get at giving up control and let chaos and the unplanned take over. I have come to learn that a two-week holiday is too short as my built-in Duracell is still moving too fast. Give me more time and I will calm down.

Recognize Long-Term Patterns

We are not born professional, we become professional through stages, is a main take away from Dreyfus and Dreyfus. During our career, we constantly get exposed to new settings, learn new things, absorb new information, react to new ideas, and unavoidably change our minds many times. My 20-, 40-, and 60-year-old self are very different persons with different professional capacities, skills, and understandings. It is all linked to the accumulation of experiences and reference points. Our problem is that we only go through this professionalizing process once. We cannot compare different paths; we only live once and will only experience the different stages once. How good it would it be if we had several parallel life tracks, so we could gain experience on the same stage twice or more. How good it would be if we at 25 could have a little experience in what it means to have 20 years' experience. But unfortunately we only get one go. On the existential level, we always move into the next professional stage unprepared. We only get recognition of long development patterns in rear view, when we already have passed the different stages, and then they are not of much help to us personally. But at least they help us to be more understanding and provide better advice when professional colleagues and friends enter the stages we already have been through. Reflexivity, accumulated experience, and pattern recognition as always provide platforms for knowledge and advice on complex issues.

Recognize Hidden Patterns

We got the Thai Government's approval to implement the constructed wetlands systems after the tsunami, despite the Thai Government stating that no international support was needed or allowed (correctly as the country easily had the capital and competence to deal with the situation) only because my Thai counterpart understood and had access to the different power pillars in the country. He took me through a long series of meetings with the Minister of Interior, the Director General of Public Infrastructure (his father), the Army General, the governors and mayors, the business leaders, and mafia bosses in the Southern Province. We even had a phone call with Thaksin, the prime minister, when he was on a plane from New York. The meetings were always polite and without content, just greetings and a cup of coffee. I had at the time no real idea of what was going on; I just knew we were trying to get a formal and informal approval of being allowed to spend the money we had received from the Danish Government. It was later I realized that we had met with all the four pillars of power, the national and provincial political leaders, the top army bosses, the influential business leaders, and key persons in the underworld, and that suddenly after all these polite meetings, we just started project implementation, despite the government's official policy. I trusted my partner, his power base, and his knowledge of how the different pillars of power had to be informed or involved, and I was correct. We never had anyone asking for anything from the project, and we encountered no objections or obstacles during implementation. We were left alone. My friend knew the game, he knew the patterns of power, he had his upper-class anchoring which gave him access to the top of all power bases, and he made the project possible to implement.

I have only this one professional friend from the upper class, and he showed me details of the power pillars in his country I had no knowledge of and no idea how they worked. He made me realize that, as a professional middle classer educated in one country, a rich country, my understanding of the underlying patterns of power in his country, which normally are hidden, especially for outsiders, were rudimentary and at times nonexistent. He made me realize that if I do not know the pillars of power in the place where I work, it can be difficult to understand what is happening around me. The pillars of power in his country were the four pillars of politics, army, business, and the underworld. The balance, struggles, and relations between these pillars determined the outcome of so many things, all the way down to how the government department we worked together in was run and by whom. These were different pillars from the ones I knew (the Danish power pillars of business, politics, and corporatism), but I realized that I needed to get a hold of them for me to provide professional advise that would make sense and could be implemented. And I realized that this need to know at times was hindered by my own morals and thinking of how power pillars should work.

Wealth distribution and the big money flows in Denmark are based on the relative strength of the Danish power pillars. The same is true for any country, but as the power pillars are different, the money flows and the actors are also different. And this can make it difficult to work in new contexts with new underlying power structures and money flows.

There are probably less than 10 countries in the world that can be labeled noncorrupt, my country of birth being one of them. Having worked in the Danish Government and the Danish private sector for more than two decades, I know this is the case; I know the mechanisms for why corruption is absent and therefore also not on the agenda of things a professional needs to know. The patterns of these informal money flows were nowhere in my nondeclarative memory. Coming from a country without, I have found that it takes time to get the inner workings and patterns of informal money flows on the backbone. My friend in Thailand, and later many other insiders, gave me better pattern recognition skills and width to this issue. When there were things I did not understand—why was this one promoted and not that one, why was the organization restructured, why was most of the budget spent in these municipalities—the logic of money normally provided the explanations. What seemed nonsensical, nonlogical, stupid, and irrational suddenly made sense—and not only internally in the organization, but also in relation to the wider context, where I started to recognize patterns of how money flowed: the police using a bottom-up approach (small distributed networked collections paying upward), the army a top-down approach (larger once-off contracts paying downward), government positions being informally tendered and appointments made on ability to pay upfront, fixed rate payment levels to upper levels based on budget size being responsible for, and so on. Each mechanism gave different actions and decisions and provided for different power relations between all involved. Each mechanism created its own world. The structure and formality of it all took me by surprise.

Such knowledge of hidden patterns and structures brings maturity in professional assessments. What seems illogical suddenly becomes clear. People and money are not stupid; there is always a rationale, and it is for the professional to understand the rationale to act professional. One thing is to understand these hidden structures theoretically; another is to understand it nonreflectively because it has been encountered, heard, and taught by insiders repeatedly. This nonreflective understanding is important as these underlying or hidden structures have so big an influence on behavior and motives, on why things happen and why not. What I have seen is that upfront payment systems derail professionalism as nobody becomes interested in the results and outcomes. But I have also seen that when professionals working inside these systems can walk on two legs, a technical output leg (we will get it done) and a money leg (we will share once done), the system works. What throws professionalism out the window is when the parties only walk on the money leg. Being professional means being professional at doing our profession. Making money is not a profession. What I have seen is that one-legged corruption basically is a way to skip the professional capability levels, skip the need to develop platforms of skills and competence, and that this type of corruption leads to easy money and arrogance. The one-legged persons I have met, be it politicians, bureaucrats, or business players, are all arrogant and have few professional skills or competences because one-legged scheming by taking money from allocated budgets is not a professional skill; anyone can do that.

What the knowledge of underlying patterns underscores is that there are always stories behind stories, layers below layers, and hidden patterns. We need to know these patterns within our professional field. And for other fields, it helps just to stay a bit skeptical, even cynical. Listen to politicians and search for the layers behind the language. Cynically read the newspaper. There is always something behind the story. When we are on the inside, we know the layers behind the story. When we are on the outside, being cynical is probably the best nonreflective starting point.

Project Story 2: Wastewater Management in Thailand—The Importance of Context

A flower and a butterfly

This project story is about context. The project highlights contextual details in a specific sector in a specific location and with all the other specifics that come with context. It shows that context is always complex, specific, and local, and what seem like pure technical issues, problems, and solutions never are. Contextual issues spill into the technical issues and make everything less straightforward. The project is anchored in the wastewater management sector.

I was outstationed to the Malaysian island of Borneo for four years as a chief technical advisor to the State Environmental Department just before the turn of the new century. We wanted to draft a regulation for wastewater treatment and decided to make an evaluation of the status of the existing systems. We found that 91 treatment plants had been constructed in the state. Of these, 89 were out of operation. The two in operation were a recently built plant, which was expected to fail soon, and a municipal pond system that was not operated by anybody, but still wastewater was flowing through by gravity and therefore it was labeled in operation! The idea of regulation fell flat as there pretty much was no treated wastewater to regulate.

Then I moved on to work as a chief technical advisor in Thailand in the newly established national wastewater management department. One of the first things I did was to visit most of the treatment plants in the country, and it quickly became clear that the situation in Thailand was similar to the one in Malaysia. Thailand had established 76 centralized systems to a cost of around two billion USD intended to treat 20 percent of the wastewater in the country through advanced activated sludge plants, stabilization ponds, and aerated lagoons. The systems had been implemented discouragingly, and the technically advanced and expensive activated sludge treatment plants were disastrous and low impact. Less than 10 treatment facilities were effectively in operation.

All these expensive, engineered centralized treatment systems were malfunctioning. It really made me wonder. As a public administration and governance specialist, I had never seen something like this before. I had never worked in a sector where, apparently, the same mistakes were repeated over and over. How could a sector, and its professional planners, engineers, and economists, accept or at least not constantly challenge such levels of failure. How could they continue to propose, design, and finance systems and technologies that already had proven not to work. However depressing it was, it was a fact. I started to get more friends and colleagues within the sector, and they all had the same stories and experiences from around the world.

Centralized wastewater management systems have a long history of sustainable operation, but only in a few rich countries. Another such system implemented here would, based on experience, have a pretty good chance of sustainability. These systems manage wastewater by full-scale trunk sewers and large centralized wastewater treatment facilities. They are based on the flush toilet, the flush-and-discharge model. These systems, when operated professionally at high costs, are efficient. This efficiency of centralized systems, unfortunately, is not seen outside the few rich countries. Here, we lack a history of a large number of successfully operated systems, we lack consistency in success of different centralized treatment technologies, and we even lack consistency for individual systems over time: What today is a successfully operated system might tomorrow become a failure, depending on some local and site-specific issues, political interference, or staff mobility. This fluidity, by the way, is one of the reasons we should be careful of professional success stories, as these are seldom *permanent* success stories; they are open-ended stories where only the future will tell the story. A revisit five years after may require some serious rewriting. That is certainly the present state of most centralized wastewater management systems implemented worldwide.

When we as professionals see failures, malfunctions, and lack of innovation, we first need to understand why. How else to act professional and contribute to better solutions.

Trying to Understand the Context

My team in Thailand, which together had decades of experience with wastewater management from different locations, perspectives, and professions, discussed why centralized technologies continued to dominate, but so seldom fit in and why it was that we, each one of us, had areas and issues we did not know, or had been told but forgot, as it was not part of our own contextual nonreflexive professional mental models. Because I found the situation grave and these professional gaps so fundamental, I wrote and got the book *Sense and Sensibility* published by ASCE,[15] the American Society of Civil Engineers. In the book, I outlined general and specific up-againsts that continue to contribute to the miseries seen in the sector.

I realized that we in the planning, construction, implementation, and operation of centralized wastewater systems are up against a wide range of complicated political, financial, historical, planning, technical, local, and even meteorological contexts that make these centralized systems fail. And I realized that these contexts are overlapping and interlinked, making it all the more difficult to grasp. We might think we have one of the contexts contributing to failure under control, but then others kick in. It all seems obvious when written down, but I guarantee you, it is not, especially when we are in the middle of it all, working hard just to reach expected outputs and achievements. It took me years to get all contexts, the combined full context, of the reasons for failure in the sector, of all the up-against, under my skin. This context complexity is why we will continue to see failures and why the next new wastewater system to be funded and constructed likely also will be an advanced expensive centralized wastewater management system, despite the track record. Let me outline some of these contexts.

The historical context. The typical picture is that in the early stages of urbanization, old irrigation systems are converted to serve as storm drains, gutters, or canals along the streets and water management is focused on flood protection rather than management of domestic effluent from households. As the urban areas densify more and more, domestic wastewater finds its way into the drainage system, and the drainage system will over time transform to combined open or covered stormwater canals and sewers. Wastewater collection systems in urban areas are therefore basically old stormwater drains that carry stormwater mixed with gray wastewater and some effluent from septic tanks, and the resulting water pollution level in these collection systems is, as a consequence, very low compared to systems where all wastewater (black and gray) is discharged directly to a closed collection system. The gradual conversion from storm to combined collection system has another implication. Open stormwater systems are designed as gravity drains with a low gradient of about 1 to 2‰. Such low gradient is insufficient for effective wastewater collection, and if no regular leakage maintenance or cleaning is carried out, only part of the wastewater will reach the centralized treatment plant.

The historical already implemented on-site wastewater management systems furthermore create complexities that are difficult to handle for new centralized systems. On-site systems (septic tanks or seepage systems) have been constructed, are in operation, and have already been paid for through private investments. These private on-site systems, and their corresponding private investments (large, when accumulated), are often ignored when public, centralized systems are planned and implemented. This normally results in conflicting coexisting systems applied simultaneously to the same areas. Linked to this is the absence of legislation enforcing private landowners to connect to a public sewer (or if the laws exist, lack of enforcement takes over). This leads to low connection rates, which again mean that the actual loading rates at centralized facilities are way lower than predicted. Many large expensive centralized systems are being implemented comprising only main and secondary sewer, but not tertiary sewer lines linking the system to the individual households. The private households are expected to pay for excavation, tearing up floors, bathrooms, or parking lots to install new pipes for the connection and redirection of gray and black wastewater flows from the private plot to the public collection system. Not strange that many do not make the effort to connect to the centralized system.

The funding context. Centralized systems lacking basic justification are by no means exceptions. Many centralized systems have no logic, except for the financial that drove their implementation. Mayors or administrators that choose not to operate centralized systems are often labeled irresponsible, careless, or antienvironmentalists, but the issue of not-making-local-sense puts the issue in a different light. Municipalities have limited budgets, and careful prioritizations must constantly be made to fulfill the many needs of the local population. In a technical rational world, it would be expected that wastewater systems are built to solve specific and significant problems and that the problems have been prioritized so the most serious problems are addressed first. But selection and prioritizing are based on many different factors, among them, of course, political and economic reasons and motivations. Centralized systems are built at a location where wastewater is not really an issue compared to many other locations. They are overdimensioned. They are unnecessarily advanced. They are built with the main purpose to spend money, as much money as the central budget or donor will and can make available. Such systems are primarily financial win–wins for the involved decision makers. And here centralized systems have big advantages over decentralized systems. They are capital heavy, easier to plan, and can be implemented in one-go.

The operation and rehabilitation context. Most centralized systems are top-down schemes financed by the central government, implemented by a contractor as a turn-key project, and then handed over to be operated and maintained by the local municipality. But operation often fails as the local municipality has neither the motivation, nor knowledge, nor the operational finances to carry out the task. When the local municipality identifies their often prohibitively expensive financial obligations to operate and maintain centralized systems, they start looking for cost savings, pumps are turned off, wastewater bypassed the treatment facility, and aerators shut down. Add to this that centralized systems need competent engineers, but the number of municipal engineers qualified to operate these systems is limited. The pool of competent engineers that find it attractive to work at a municipal wastewater treatment facility with uncompetitive salaries and uncertain budgets is even more limited. Wastewater management is low on the job wish-list of engineers, much lower than other engineering disciplines, and the municipality can quickly find itself in a situation where it does not have enough professional staff to operate the system.

Those attempting to improve operation, maintenance, and rehabilitation of such existing centralized systems, which was one of the aims of the project I was in charge of, soon find the task difficult, if not impossible. The fundamental problems mean that rehabilitation becomes much more than an issue of technical upgrading of skills and rehabilitation of broken infrastructure or missing equipment. The contextual problems are deep and most often cannot be solved when other pressing issues exist and when the priorities of the municipality are not in favor of the required allocation of energy, resources, and competence to rehabilitate and operate the centralized system.

The planning context. The planning of efficient centralized systems is up against serious uncertainties and unreliable data. The professional wastewater management planner will almost always get it wrong. When we plan and design centralized systems, we need to know the present and future number of people, the number of connections, average water consumptions, the water/wastewater ratio, the black/gray wastewater ratio, the average leakages and infiltration rates, the average loading rates, and the present and future costs, just to mention the most important. From these data, we can predict needs and design wastewater collection and treatment systems. Everyone with practical experience will know that each of the aforementioned data requirements, which might appear simple and straightforward, often are very difficult to get a hold on. The collection of baseline data is far from a simple issue of calling different agencies or looking in the official statistics and then proceeding from there. Add to this that many urban areas are developing rapidly and that these rapid growth rates often are uneven not only between subdistricts but also between seasons with huge rural–urban or tourism-based flows, creating a whole new bunch of problems for the wastewater management planner.

All these uncertainties typically result in the planner overdimensioning the treatment facility to be on the safe side. But the low connection rates, the lack of laws to force connection, sewers being drainage systems mainly carrying gray wastewater diluted with rainwater, and the complexity and leakages of the existing collection system lead to grossly overdimensioned centralized treatment systems unnecessarily equipped to function with high organic loading rates, which lead to scrapped or inefficient treatment facilities, unused equipment, treatment units closed to reduce energy costs, or malfunctioning treatment processes.

The planner also struggles to solve the significant problems of high and fluctuating rainfalls and wet and dry seasons. Areas with intensive shock loadings of rainwater create highly fluctuating loading rates at the central treatment facilities and serious first flush problems (the first heavy rain after a dry period), where vast amounts of heavily polluted sludge, which have been accumulated in the sewers during the long dry period, of necessity, is made to bypass the treatment facility and flushed untreated into rivers and coastal areas. These heavy rains also result in huge amounts of soil being flushed down hills, choking the collection system and making central treatment systems malfunctioning.

Systems lacking overall justifications, local operation of central initiated and implemented facilities, overdimensioned and too advanced systems, the complexity of the collection system, the low connection and loading rates, the lack of climate fitness are all reasons that result in the high number of malfunctioning centralized systems.

The local political, educational, legislative, institutional, and financial frameworks determine the success of centralized systems, and in many locations, these frameworks are inadequate for the introduction of advanced centralized systems. In a few rich countries, these underlying systems have been developed over many decades or even centuries, continuously becoming more complex and coherent as the public sector became economically and organizationally stronger.

But an equally interesting point is that it might not only be a question of preparedness for centralized systems, but rather a question of the *appropriateness* of these systems, because to be appropriate means to take the local context seriously, to understand the context and plan the most appropriate system, to assess the site in terms of population, climate, character of wastewater, efficiency of existing or previous systems, connection rates, laws and regulations, enforcement practices, local support and habits, political preferences, incentives, local lessons learned, and so on. The local context is a large and complex diffuse cloud of multiple local parameters that together form the contextual frame of an appropriate system.

Many locations have not yet made investments in centralized systems, giving opportunities for experiments with new and more suitable concepts that fit the local context better. In periods where traditional paradigms prove insufficient, and new have yet to fully take form, many new emerging views, opinions, and competing systems and technologies see the day of light. Some of these are more appropriate than others, and as for all technical problems, not only one solution exists.

I had a discussion with my team on what we thought characterizes appropriate wastewater management systems. The outright technical winner was stand-alone on-site wastewater systems where wastewater is managed (produced, treated, and reused) on-site. Wastewater is here treated on-site to a level making it suitable for infiltration through the natural soil matrix and thus recharged back to the water cycle through groundwater sources. Domestic wastewater is rarely a major problem if it is not collected, concentrated, and discharged at a single outlet. But whether on-site, cluster, or centralized system is implemented, the runner-up was that it must always be possible to operate and maintain the system locally. Thereafter came the use of short, gravity-based, separated wastewater collection systems. Then came the reuse of treated wastewater and integration into the urban environment. Finally came the utilization of smart technologies.

I developed and included in my book checklists for the contextual reasons for failure and contextual appropriateness to help professionals not forget the big contextual picture. The checklists work as design criteria or guidelines in the planning process and as checklists upon which the level of appropriateness can be evaluated. The more contextual checks a system gets, the more likely it will succeed as a local contextual-efficient and site-optimized response to wastewater challenges.

As for any professional checklist, the application of checklists has both a *technical and a depth side*. The *technical side* is the number of appropriate checks achieved and the number of contextual dangers avoided. They are spottable; they can be seen and ticked off: Have they been applied—yes, no, or only partially? But a good appropriate system is not a simple question of ticking of a yes, no, or partial. It is a question of being the best and most appropriate system for this problem at this location at this time, with these users and managers with their competencies, interests, motivations, and resources. It means that the most appropriate system always includes important choices and judgments: Which elements should be included, which left out? Have all alternatives been carefully considered before we justifiably gave up on an element? This is the complex matter of *depth* in appropriateness, in the choices of planning and design, in the contextual assessment. A specific system appropriateness depends on our ability to assess. And our ability to assess, design, plan, and implement depends on the depth of our own professional experience.

I found that the two issues of *sense and simplicity* define and frame appropriateness, and thereby also good professionals. Any system must make *sense* for the local decision makers, financial contributors, taxpayers, or owners. Making sense is key for local fitness, appropriateness, and sustainability. The tricky thing is that it almost always makes sense for someone, for the central governments providing the finance, for the engineer being expert in the activated sludge technology, and for the coastal ecosystem environmentalist. And still, the numerous malfunctioning systems indicate a lack of making sense of who is supposed to continue operation, maintenance, and financing the system. The key is if the system makes sense for the mayor, municipal director, the owner of the on-site system, the ones responsible for financing, operation, and maintenance; will they find the costs, resources, and inputs required to make the system work justifiably compared to alternative uses of the resources and finances available.

Simplicity is the other key factor for local fitness, appropriateness, and sustainability. Simplicity implies simplifying the management system, the technology, and the details. Simplicity is to reduce the level of complexity as much as possible and to cut the number of elements that can eventually lead to the failure of the system. Is pond treatment sufficient, could the number of pumps be reduced, is this component necessary, could the intake structure be built simpler with fewer mechanical components? Every time process complexity is reduced, the need for maintenance, the cost for replacements, and the required technical operational knowledge are also reduced, and the chances for system sustainability increased.

Risking My Neck: The Flower and the Butterfly

At the end of my three-year assignment in Thailand, the Indian Ocean tsunami of 2004 struck and my team and I were afforded an opportunity to test some of our experiences in praxis, as we together with the national wastewater department took it on us to reconstruct three damaged wastewater treatment facilities in the south of Thailand. Under the leadership of the political astute Deputy Director General, Sarawut Srisakuna, the wastewater authority with my team of national and international experts was allocated a tsunami reconstruction budget from the Danish Government through the embassy in Bangkok.

One of the rehabilitation projects was on the island of Koh Phi Phi located on the west coast of southern Thailand. One hour by boat from Phuket, you arrive on a tropical island in the heart of a national marine park. Two mountainous islands covered by rain forest rise vertically above sea level. The two rocks are connected by a narrow sand dune, about one-kilometer long and 200 meters wide, creating two beautiful U-shaped lagoons and making the contour of the island look like the shape of a butterfly. The mountainous parts are preserved as a part of the national park, whereas the sand strip has been developed by private landowners.

Some thousand kilometers from the island, two tectonic plates deep below the Indian Ocean created a powerful tidal wave traveling with a speed of 800 kilometers per hour in the direction of Thailand. At high speed, a huge wave bent around the western mountain of Koh Phi Phi and struck the island first from the south and then from the north. Soon after, a second and even more devastating wave hit the island. Within minutes, most structures on the densely built-up strip of land were flattened; bungalows, shops, and restaurants in ruins; and 600 lives lost. The tsunami left Koh Phi Phi devastated with its businesses and infrastructures destroyed. Utility networks, roads, water supply, electrical power supply, and the wastewater system were all in ruins. The Thai Government allowed only a few projects to be funded through international donations; one was the grant from the Danish Government for the rehabilitation of the wastewater management system at Koh Phi Phi for which I was the project manager.

During the first decades of Koh Phi Phi's development into a major tourist destination, all buildings on the island were equipped with seepage wells, and all wastewater was treated and discharged within the plot. As time went by, the increased densification of the sand strip and the limited availability of land resulted in the on-site systems reaching a critical mass. In the early 1990s, a group of government authorities, consultants, and contractors arrived on the island. They funded and built a centralized collection and treatment system and left the island. The wastewater treatment plant was never put into operation. For a decade, the municipality had two large treatment ponds fenced behind barbed wires that did not receive any wastewater, mainly because part of the gravity-based collection system had been constructed with a negative slope. The wastewater decomposed under the streets causing smell and, during rains, flooded onto the streets. Reality was the opposite of a tropical paradise. The municipality reacted by implementing a by-law *prohibiting* people from discharging wastewater to the centralized collection system. Without flow through the system, the collection system was slowly filled with sand.

When centralized government systems fail, people try to manage and solve their problems themselves. A local hotel and landowner took over and implemented a second, independent, and parallel collection and treatment system on her own land, which was around half the island. She had completed the collection system, and an advanced wastewater treatment at the end of the collection system was under construction when the tsunami hit the island.

After the tsunami, the private wastewater collection system remained partly intact, whereas the treatment system was completely devastated. The local entrepreneur was about to rehabilitate the system, when the idea of joining hands with our municipal-led rehabilitation project emerged. The hotel owner saved the expenses for building a new treatment plant and we were given access to a well-functioning collection system, which would ensure adequate loadings at the treatment plant. Local public hearings and meetings with all key stakeholders provided the go-ahead for the project. At the first meeting we had with the mayor, he stressed that they wanted a new system that did not smell, looked beautiful, would be easy and cheap to operate, and requested that a five-year operation and maintenance contract should be included in the contract with the Danish Embassy as the international donor. All requirements closely linked to the previous experiences on the island. The mayor had made regional trips to study best practices and had a personal liking for constructed wetlands as a treatment technology. We tried our utmost to fulfill his and the community's wishes.

And I think we made them proud as we designed and built one of the most beautiful wastewater treatment plants in the world, *The Flower and the Butterfly*, a recovery-based closed-loop wastewater management system. We wanted to contribute to innovation, and in this, we succeeded as the Koh Phi Phi constructed wetlands became one of the world's most cited wastewater management systems. My professional team of wastewater experts toured the world, still do, with their nice PowerPoint presentations. The treatment facility was designed to symbolize a butterfly sitting on a flower with a symbolic reference to the butterfly-shaped contour of Koh Phi Phi. The relationship between the flower and the butterfly symbolized a new beginning, the growth and bloom of the flower, the community and the island in the aftermath of the tsunami.

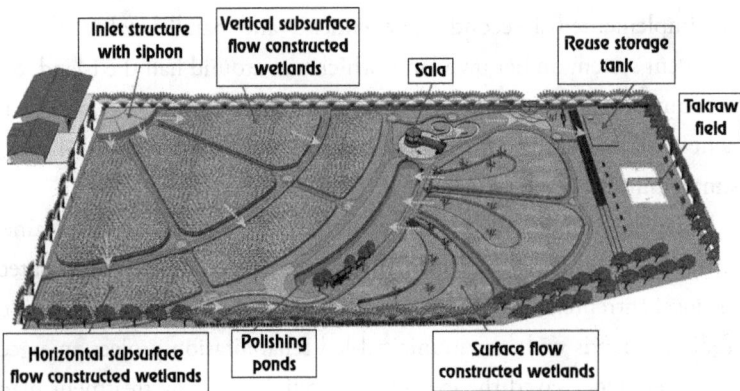

Flower and butterfly treatment plant design

Flower and butterfly treatment plant final

On constructing a wastewater treatment facility on a small tropical island, the issues of simplicity, user friendliness, robustness, ease of operation and maintenance, low-energy consumption, and aesthetics become evident. We were given 12 months to design and construct the system and we made it on time, and budget. The project presented the essence of what we regarded appropriate cluster wastewater management.

The treatment system. The basic principle behind the constructed wetlands is magical, simple, and effective: Wastewater passes through gravel filters, which by natural microorganic processes treat the wastewater. The gravel filters we implemented were one meter deep, consisted of three layers of gravels in different sizes, and was underlaid with an impermeable synthetic liner. At the top of the filtering gravel media, we planted effective removal vegetation, such as the beautiful heliconia and cannae lilies. Our treatment plant treated wastewater in a robust mix of four different treatment technologies. In the first of the three types of gravel filter constructed wetlands we used, the *vertical subsurface* system (the first three petals of the flower), the wastewater was evenly distributed to the full surface of the gravel filter through an inlet reservoir powered by three large-scale siphons. The siphons were used to ensure even distribution of the wastewater to the full surface of the gravel filter through a distri-bution pipe system located on top of the gravel filter. From the outlet at the bottom of the first system, the water flows into the three lines of the *horizontal subsurface* system (the next three petals of the flower), where the wastewater flows horizontally below the surface through the gravel filter to the outlet at the other end. From here, it flows into the *horizontal surface* system, where it flows on the surface of the gravel filter (the three wings of the butterfly), before the wastewater is led into a *polishing pond* (the body of the butterfly) and then discharged fully treated to the reuse reservoir. The flow of wastewater from start to finish is based on gravity.

The urban integration system. The site of the treatment facility was surrounded by bungalows and resorts and along one side ran the main path connecting the eastern and western side of the island. With such high visibility, unorthodox design ideas were required. At the very beginning, we were up against a solid misbelief about any planning of a centralized wastewater system as this was already tested and failed. There-fore, considerable efforts were spent to optimize and integrate the design into the landscape of the island, to look beautiful, be underground, look simple, natural, and probably, for most, also surprising: Can wastewater really be treated this way? Not only does the system collect, treat, and reuse the wastewater on the island, it also functions as a public park with walk paths, benches, and a pavilion. Everyone can enter the park and enjoy the blooming heliconia flowers, besides being informed about the treatment processes in the system.

The collection system. We upgraded the existing collection system so that storm water run-off became managed in an independent open drain-age system, while the closed wastewater collection system was established to minimize the risk of wastewater reaching the streets during heavy showers, preventing sand from entering and blocking the pipes, reducing maintenance costs, and minimizing dilution to ensure a homogenous level of constituents that optimized treatment effectiveness. All wastewater was collected in the closed system by gravity to a single location in the central part of the town from where the wastewater was pumped to the treatment facility through a pressure pipe, again to avoid leakage and smell. As there was no law forcing households to connect to public wastewater collec-tion systems, tertiary household service pipes and connection works were included in the construction contract. The contract also included oil and grease traps for households, restaurants, and hotels. Thai cooking is heavy on oils that messes up both the collection and treatment systems.

The energy system. To reduce energy consumption, the pumping station in the town center was equipped with solar panels and battery storage to support the operation of the pumps. Additional required power was supplied from the electricity grid on the island. The treatment facility intake system used large-scale siphons instead of an electrical pump, thereby reducing consumption as the siphons work entirely on hydraulic principle without power supply.

The reuse system. The reclaimed water was reused for irrigation of green areas on the treatment facility itself, along public paths and in the surrounding private resorts. The reuse provided for a cyclic land-based re-entry system, which was important for a location that otherwise could only discharge directly onto and into one of the two beautiful tropical beaches.

The organizational and financial system. The construction of the project was carried out by a local contractor, who hired members of the *local community committee* as advisors and middle managers. This ensured knowledge of the local context, local suppliers, and pricing, while developing local knowledge on the functionality of the system. A wastewater management committee with the mayor, the local community leader, and representatives from the business community was established. As I expected that the wastewater system during the first year of operation would experience operation and maintenance issues, some from the construction works, some from the always-required adjustments and operational run-in of especially a biological and innovative treatment facility as the one on Koh Phi Phi, I managed to establish safeguards for the first five years of operation: first, a one-year 10 percent performance bond which secured and enabled the municipality and donor to require the contractor to rectify any construction mistakes or omissions observed; second, a three-year postsupervision contract with a national technical expert to closely follow and supervise operation and maintenance issues, report to the municipality and donor for action to be taken to secure efficient operation; and third, as part of the total construction budget, a five-year half a million USD donor-funded municipal operation and maintenance budget to provide the municipality with ample time to include the full operation and maintenance costs onto its normal municipal budget.

That is how the Koh Phi Phi system was designed, implemented, and came to look. Everyone involved was proud, and tired. The rapid design, construction, and operational upstart period required so much energy that it drained all involved. But we did it.

Postevaluation

We worked as a team and we achieved the implementation of the Koh Phi Phi treatment plant as a team. I was part of it all from the big to the small and as a project manager I learned the importance of context and new aspects of the four implementation agendas, lessons that further developed my professional depth. Surrounding any project is its specific context with its specific TPPU issues, and we must learn this context in detail if we want to be good professional project managers. It is in the specifics and details that we get sufficient depth.

I learned that without knowing the local context, we must be humble and, always, must ask and listen. Koh Phi Phi represents a paradox. It is a showcase, but should not be copied to other small islands, as centralized systems and small islands are not a good fit. Still, we implemented a centralized cluster system! Koh Phi Phi had already implemented a centralized system and our first intention was to rehabilitate this system. Coming to the island immediately after the tsunami, we quickly realized that this system had never been working. Back to square one and investigating the possibilities of on-site collection and treatment. But then real on-the-ground decentralized design problems started. The area to be covered was the dense business and hotel district consisting of two-storied business complexes and a six-floor hotel complex. This area was compact and dense, mixed orderly and chaotic. Most buildings had problems with their seepage system, either because they had no land around the house, had no way of reallocating the septic tank that was constructed under the house, or were located very close to the sea with high groundwater levels making seepage difficult. Now what? If a decentralized system was chosen, this could not include the area of the large landowner, as she had already established and paid for a centralized cluster system.

And it could not include many of the remaining buildings due to technical problems with density and seepage. With a decentralized on-site system, maybe only 25 buildings could be supported. Back to the drawing board again. Could the well-functioning and already established centralized but private cluster wastewater collection system be utilized? Could a win–win situation with the landowner be created? Would she allow other residents to connect to her collection system? Would the mayor approve of the idea, especially of the idea of combining a private collection system with the municipal treatment plant? Things started to take shape, handshakes made, details discussed and agreed upon, and suddenly a design began to take form. And it was, again, a centralized cluster system. Experts from outside, not knowing this intricate local context, could easily point fingers: How could you?

I learned I had to take technical decisions, even in areas where I was not the expert. When designing wastewater systems, numerous technical issues surface. I experienced this all too clearly in our design phase. Twelve international and national wastewater experts were involved, some of them world-renowned experts within this field, and it would be wrong to say they agreed on everything. The gravel media, shapes, inlet structures, size and type of inlet pipes, and lining, almost everything was up for discussion. This normally indicates, to use Kuhn's term, a new paradigm still searching for the optimal, in contrast to an established paradigm, where the technology is well defined. I knew this, the technical experts likely not; they just argued and discussed, over and over, until I took a decision: let us go for a gravel diameter of 12 mm instead of 14 mm in the second gravel layer!

I learned that most technical issues involve serious balancing of cost and benefits. The benefit of vertical constructed wetland systems is that they are twice as efficient as horizontal flow systems. Or, in other words, they can treat twice as much wastewater on the same area. As increased wastewater quantities were foreseen, and as land scarcity was a real issue, the treatment capacity had to be optimized as much as possible. But as usual, benefits come with costs, the cost being increased complexity in design and operation, and thereby increased risk of failure. The main difference is the more *complex distribution system in the vertical system.* The factor to secure higher efficiency is the even distribution of water on the whole surface. This is achieved through multiple outlets on manifold pipes. But the sheer number of outlets presents an operational and efficiency risk. Outlets can become blocked or unbalanced and then not discharge evenly. It should not go wrong, but it can! We decided to include both systems. As this was one of the first constructed wetland systems in the country and as the location was so prominent, all had the ambition to make the site a demonstration site for the constructed wetland technology, and for applying different constructed wetland technologies at one site. Similar cost–benefit considerations played out for the layout of the treatment plant. Six different layouts were made in the design phase. Each type of configuration had benefits and disadvantages; for costs, effectiveness, land utilization, or landscaping. A round shape is good for vertical systems, as it provides the smallest distance from each outlet to the water distribution box resulting in less risk for pressure loss and uneven distribution. Rectangular shapes are good for horizontal systems as they provide a better control of the flow. An uneven shape, as a flower or butterfly shape, provides for better urban integration and beautification, but gives larger distances to the distribution box and less straight water flows. A choice had to be made, and in this case, the technical arguments were slightly overridden by the need for urban integration, landscaping, and beautification. But only to some extent, as the flowers basically were made in a rectangular form, and we expected the flower to do the major part of the treatment work as water quality would be below national standards already after leaving the flower. This allowed for more room, creativity, and odd forms in the configuration of the subsequent treatment processes, which then came to look like a butterfly.

I learned that with sector paradigm shifts come risks. We knew the project needed to mix and match treatment technologies to become most efficient. We were certain the constructed wetland treatment technology would work its magic. Still, are constructed wetlands a proven technology? If proven is defined as proven to work, the answer is yes. Experiments, pilot and demonstration projects, in many locations under different conditions all over the world have provided enough evidence for the efficiency of the technology. But if proven is defined as having been applied and operated with success for decades, large scale, and in all possible locations, then no. The technology is a newcomer in applied wastewater management. Still, I found the technology had proven its usefulness and appropriateness and the time had come to go from experiments to larger-scale application of constructed wetlands: A minister or governor deciding that wastewater management in the country or province should increasingly be based on constructed wetlands. This would move the technology out of the experimental closet into the real life of financing and treatment of wastewater. And real comparisons and improvement of factors like effectiveness, sustainability, and robustness could begin. I wanted to contribute to that overall context and development.

I learned to focus on making sense and create win–win situations. The reasons for why wastewater should be treated were obvious for all landowners and residents on the island. The project certainly passed the *does it make sense* test. The winner in wastewater treatment is often thought of as the environment. In creating sustainable wastewater management systems, however, this is rarely enough. Win–win situations must be found and created for as many stakeholders as possible. Even though motivations are personal and hidden, and therefore often not so easy to predict or get right, some of the win–win situations I consciously tried to establish included: *The mayor.* Who knows what a mayor gets out of it, but one thing is for sure: If it is nothing, the project would not have happened. *The contractor*, besides an opportunity to make some money, also saw the project as an opportunity to enter a new market—*the key hotel and landowner* saving costs by linking to the new treatment plant. *The local community leader* was hired by the contractor as supervisor. He was later in charge of operation and maintenance. *The local residents* were relieved of the increasingly difficult problem of finding new locations for their seepage systems. *The national authority, international and local experts, and me* were all provided with a chance to work together and design, innovate, and bring to full scale an interesting project within our professional field—*and* the governor, the Ministry of Natural Resources and Environment, the National and Provincial Public Works Departments, the company back home, the Danish Embassy, the participating universities, the subsuppliers, the gravel freight company, and so on. The number of players involved in design, approvals, tendering, contracting, and implementation is diverse and numerous. A key factor for success and sustainability, and a key task for a project manager, is that all involved actors at the end gain something from having participated in the project.

I learned to use interdependency and exposure as implementation tools. As project manager, I tried to develop as many interdependable relations as possible. The contractor dependent on the mayor, the mayor accountable to the governor, the consultants dependent on their reputation, the community leader responsible to the powerful landowners, and so on. These links strengthen the project and its chances for success. And I used exposure. A system built and failed in the backyard of a small municipality in the middle of nowhere attracts little attention. A system that has been exposed, being exceptional in design, presented in newspapers, and professional magazines, that has visitors from the ministries or from technical experts from all over will be more difficult to let fail. We lose face if we have told our peers, constituents, or bosses that it will work.

I learned to think in up-againsts and safeguards. At the time I had enough experience to know that the Koh Phi Phi wastewater management system could fail. Wastewater management systems in Thailand are up against a troubling track record. On islands, they are up against island cultures of small communities with shifting strong and weak community leaders and high degrees of corruption and in-fighting. On Koh Phi Phi, they are up against a long history of malfunctioning, nonoperated, nonmaintained infrastructure projects, not only wastewater, but also energy supply, water supply, and solid waste management. Through the financial safeguards, local anchoring, commitment, and exposure, I tried my best to safeguard the project.

I learned that things still can go wrong. The job was done, the system worked, it was handed over at a big ceremony, my contract came to an end, and I left the project, returned home, and with the financial, technical, and operational safeguards in place, I expected the municipality would operate and maintain the plant without too many problems. As expected, the plant did face some operational issues during its first year. These were related to high biochemical oxygen demand (BOD) loading, high levels of oil and grease, and operational problems with the solar-powered pumps; issues that if managed and solved efficiently and fastly would not provide serious problems for the system. This, however, and not as expected, did not happen. The municipality did not actively take responsibility for management and problem solving, and the donor did not activate the safeguards.

The supervision budget for the local expert was utilized as planned, but the issues raised in his postsupervision reports, which should be rectified by the contractor, the municipality, and the embassy were not resolved. The financial and technical tools were in place, but time and energy were wasted on reports and discussions without actions being taken to rectify the observed and manageable operation and maintenance issues. The performance bond was not activated to make the contractor rectify the reported issues. The embassy did not release the operational budgets set aside. The municipal committee did not function as planned. The mayor went absent. The national wastewater department was 2,000 km away. Issues were left unattended. I sat in my office in Denmark and could do nothing but listen. When I left, my force field left with me. No decisions or actions were taken, everything was left in a limbo, and then the small operation problems piled up and morphed into a different type of problem—into blame game problems, where things go legal, everything becomes negotiations and processes of responsibilities, and nobody acts.

I knew of these issues because the local expert hired by the Danish Embassy, Dr. Thammarat Kootatep from the Asian Institute of Technology (AIT), was my good friend. He still is. He told me of the stalemate, the nonactions by the embassy, and the lack of budget to remedy the issues. Instead of solving the practical low-budget issues, the embassy chose to sue my company for lack of engineering design drawings and technical specifications. I had seen our role as technical advisors to the government, not construction engineers. I thought this was a Thai project with the national and local authorities being responsible. The embassy thought differently. This process took a couple of years, my company negotiated a fee to be paid, and nothing happened on the ground. It became an issue between Danes. Nobody asked the national department or the municipality for anything.

Two years passed, I got information from Thammarat, but because I could do nothing, I think he knew this story made me so angry and depressed and we stopped sharing information on the project. I moved on and left the project behind with the assumption that it had become yet another one of the failed wastewater projects in Thailand.

I wrote this in my book *Sense and Sensibility* two years after completion:

Case-stories will always be stories in real time, and therefore only present a snapshot of the situation as the time of writing. The real world consists of ever-evolving processes, and in one, two or three months or years from now the situation and context will have changed, and so will the case story. How the Koh Phi Phi case story, like all other case stories, will evolve is rather impossible to predict. I can just hope that the ever-changing mix of stakeholders will be able to cooperate and together find the energy, time and resources required to manage and counter both the big up-against's and the present nitty-gritties for the sustainable operation and maintenance of the Koh Phi Phi treatment system.[16]

I learned that some play power games unknown to me. The Danish Ambassador to Thailand played a painful power game on me. At the end of implementation, when the project looked beautiful and started to attract attention, the embassy called me to ask if I could arrange an on-site visit for the Ambassador, whom I had never met during the previous three years, reporting directly to the embassy. He came for three days; we showed him around and had a good time. He returned to Bangkok and I never saw or talked to him again. When the project ran into its first year operational issues, the Ambassador refused to release the operational budgets set aside, but chose instead to launch an attack on my company back in Copenhagen. He activated the full force of the Ministry of Foreign Affairs' legal department. As the Ambassador never contacted me to discuss what the issues were or how they could be solved, I can only guess about his motives. Having worked later as a diplomat, I guess the reason was the cover-my-back strategy, applied almost instinctively in the extremely risk-averse Foreign Affairs sector. Blame someone else to be sure you cannot be blamed thereby not being promoted or transferred to the next country. Who knows. Having my company pay a fee for something that could rather easily have been solved was painful. It was particularly painful because I was not offered a position to fight from. He was a small man. And an outlier. I learned the hard way that I had nothing to learn from his power game but should continue to concentrate on all the normal professionals where trust, fairness, and cooperation are in focus.

But luckily, I also learned that things can work out in the end if other force fields take over. Ten years after I had left the project, one late evening, I received an e-mail from Thammarat. It had an attachment which he said I would find interesting. He is a modest guy. The attachment was a technical paper he had published in an international wastewater magazine. It had page after page of wastewater calculations, formulas, data, and graphs. It contained years of effluent monitoring results for BOD, chemical oxygen demand, total dissolved solids, and total suspended solids, the parameters used to monitor how efficient a treatment facility is working. It concluded that the treatment plant for the last eight years had achieved treatment levels within the national standards for wastewater treatment. The monitored wastewater plant was the Koh Phi Phi wastewater treatment facility! After my initial shock and disbelief, I called him. He told me that after all the negativity and lack of release of the allocated five-year budget from the Danish Embassy, he had approached the Japanese Embassy and asked if they could provide technical and operational assistance. They agreed, and he managed to get all important stakeholders on board again. The community leader got employed as caretaker and he had managed the plant efficiently ever since. He got AIT students to monitor treatment efficiency. He made the "mix of stakeholders cooperate and together find the energy, time and resources required to manage and counter both the big up-against's and the present nitty-gritties for the sustainable operation and maintenance of the Koh Phi Phi treatment system."[17] He became the project's new force field. He made it happen. I slept well that night.

CHAPTER 5

Anchors

We become poor professionals when we do not know our anchors and the big picture we are part of, when our efforts are based in wrong mental models, and when the big picture, the view from the many, has changed without we noticing it. Then, we are in real trouble if we think we know what we are talking about.

We are always part of larger contexts, some we understand, but not all as it can be difficult to grasp big picture contexts from our own small point of view. I have come to think that the five anchors and big picture contexts covered in this chapter are the most important to get a hold of to become good project managers and good professionals. Understanding these anchors helps us connect the dots. To understand the broader context that anchors us take effort and slow thinking as these understandings are derived from platforms we cannot get a hold off from our own small experience-based point of view. They require good mental models that help us consolidate contexts, complexity, the view from the many, big picture knowledge into generalized representations we can grasp and remember. Mental models are remembering tools and the following five anchors of organization, sector, globalization, demographic, and evolution are hopefully memorable mental models for what anchors us and what we must know to become professionals. These anchors matter as they frame our capacities in complex systems; they frame contexts we need to know to become and act professional. They also tell us what to expect.

Anchor 1: Know Your Organization

A key and important context for professionals is the organizational structure we belong to or operate within. We all operate in organizations where all professionals must also be organizational experts. If we cannot operate professionally in the specific organizational type we are part of, we will struggle. If we want to be entrepreneurial in a machine organization, we will fail. If we demand detailed control structures in entrepreneurial organizations, we will get disappointed. We need to have specific knowledge of and expectations to the *specific* organization we are anchored in. In the first decade of our professional career, circumstances and organizations normally choose us. Later, with more professional experience in the bag, we realize that there are different types of organizations we can be part of and that some of these fit us better than others. And we, at this stage, sometimes have the chance to choose. In a perfect world, we should then find the most appropriate type of organization, the organization type that matches our preferences and skills, and then anchor our professional efforts there. But life is not perfect or fair for that matter, and it is often not for us to choose which organization we end up in. But at least we should know the characteristics of the types of organizations that anchor our professional career.

Some of the things we have experienced or read stick because they had and still have relevance. Take Mintzberg's organizational structures,[1] which I was taught in the sixth semester at university and later taught to sixth semester students, and which I still remember today and use as a mental model to understand and frame the organizations I have worked in or advised. Mintzberg reminds us that there are different species of organizations, and we should not mix them up. Hospitals are not factories, advertising agencies not fast-food companies, and engineering consultancy companies not entrepreneurial companies. This may seem obvious, but we often mix up the different species of organizations. Our vocabulary for understanding organizations is quite primitive. The reason there are different species of organizations is of course that an organization's structure makes a real difference to the way it performs. That is why some companies achieve success through strict controls, while others achieve success through loose-coupled structures.

I have, in the last decade, run my own entrepreneurial company; I have worked 15 years in a global project-based engineering company, 12 years in three different public professional bureaucracies, and early on I worked in a couple of machine organizations. That pretty much covers Mintzberg's spectrum of different types of organizations. I have experienced first-hand that each of these organizational types provides very different platforms for professionals and very different types of restrictions and opportunities.

We can find ourselves working in an *entrepreneurial organization* with its simple, flat, loose structure driven by entrepreneurial minded managers, who often are also the owners. Forward-thinking ideas, energy, a strong defined sense of mission, enthusiasm, and the ability to take quick, decisive action are common strengths. The drawbacks are limited structure, inefficiency, and overcontrolling owner managers, as all important decisions tend to be centralized in the hands of the owner. I know these opportunities and constraints all too well through the experiences I give the professionals that join my entrepreneurial company. All entrepreneurial organizations face tough decision when they succeed and grow, and we can get stuck in the deep transition problems this creates. Because of the growth, the organization transitions into a different type of organization with HR, marketing, legal departments, and all. But most entrepreneurial companies struggle with these transitions because many owner managers cannot cope with the transition into a big, orderly, and structured organization with many decision makers, and many therefore self-destruct, disintegrate, or vanish. One heart attack can wipe out the whole entrepreneurial organization.

Some will be working in an *ad hoc project-based organization* characterized by the constant launching of projects to respond quickly and flexibly to changing demands. Research laboratories, filmmaking, consulting, advertising agencies, high-tech industries, and pharmaceuticals use such a project-based structure. Contrary to the entrepreneurial organization, decision making is here decentralized and determined by skilled professionals that are brought together to form an ad hoc functional team to tackle a project. Professionals typically move from team to team and from project to project, as projects are completed and new projects develop. The project-based decentralized decision-making structure can be difficult to control or manage, as the potential for leadership conflict, authority uncertainty, and ambiguous power relations are ever present. And job security is an issue as the structure is fully dependent on constantly winning and funding new projects. Not for the faint-hearted.

Many professionals will be working in a *professional bureaucracy*, an organization where highly trained professionals are given autonomy and control in the organization. Schools, hospitals, universities, accounting and law firms, and engineering companies exemplify this structure. The professional bureaucracy is bureaucratic without being centralized and is based on clear lines of authority and standard administrative practices. The professional bureaucracy is about proficiency more than efficiency. The critical work is highly skilled and can take years of training, yet most of the time, it can be surprisingly routine. Professionals are usually working on their own, carrying out own procedures according to the predetermined protocols. By their nature, professional bureaucracies are hard to manage because authority and power are spread down through the hierarchy. The professionals within the company want to make their own decisions and want a say in decisions that affect them, so the decision-making process tends to be long, complicated, and difficult to complete. But professional bureaucracies typically are stable, are robust, and hardly change over time.

And finally, we can find ourselves working in a *machine organization* with its high levels of work standardization and its units working together like the parts of a machine. Tasks are standardized and detailed in operating procedures. The machine organization has a rigid hierarchical structure, lines of authority are formal, there are rules to follow, and communication needs to follow a structure and adhere to reporting lines. Large-scale manufacturing plants, highly bureaucratic government agencies, and large set-in-their-ways corporations epitomize this style. These organizations are efficient and rely heavily on economies of scale for their success. Efficiency is the name of the game, and the managers are mainly concerned with fine-tuning their bureaucratic machine. Professional managers with their planning and standardization at all levels rule the organization.

Having worked in all these different organizational structures, I have experienced that Mintzberg's mental model is valuable. I have seen professionals getting depressed or disappointed by expecting something from an organization that it cannot deliver. I have seen the complications of trying to move a company from being an entrepreneurial to a machine company, expecting the entrepreneurial owner to suddenly comply with structures and rules of internal departments. I have seen professionals moving from a political organization to a private sector business environment, expecting that the culture change can be overcome easily. Many of the problems arising from leaps between types of organizations are predictable and often sad as they come with high personal consequences and losses.

I have also seen the use of the wrong tools in the wrong type of organizations. I have undertaken more than 80 project evaluations, and it took me some time to realize that most of these were a waste of effort, time, and money. The idea that we plan, implement, and evaluate is good, but some organizations—foreign aid organizations, foreign affairs, political parties to mention a few—are simply not geared to or interested in structured technical evaluation of their previous plans and use of money. Their goal posts move all the time, their focus is on present and future plans and budgets, which all depend on the present intensive power struggles. Almost all of the evaluation reports I have spent tons of hours preparing, conceptualizing, and carefully writing down was read by only me and my team.

Mintzberg, by the way, also described in detail the trajectory of organizations turning into monopolies. Sometimes, we expect of private, government, or political organizations that have achieved to become monopolies that they can self-correct the down sides of being a monopoly; we think they can control their power arrogance, bureaucratic decay, lack of innovation, stagnation, and corruption. They cannot. In South Africa, the political party ANC has been a political monopoly for more than 25 years, and everything in its present downfall follows to the tee Mintzberg's script for decay, corruption, and disintegration of monopolies. Nothing else could have been expected, even though how much we wished it was not so.

My exposure to different organizational types has also given me insight into some of the more generic characteristics of organizations and organizational life. I have seen that *organizations are never only technical rational*. When I enter an organization, sometimes as an analytical organizational consultant, I do no longer expect to see a rational decision-making machine. I know I will see an organization of many people and groups with different and often contradictory objectives and preferences, I will find important organizational actors both inside and outside the formal organizational structure, and I will find aims and objectives clouded in ambiguity. The decision-making and planning activities will resemble more an ad hoc emergency planning than blueprint planning, and responses to unexpected pressures will often override everything else.

I have also seen that *decisions taken can be very difficult to understand* as decisions are taken for many different reasons based on many different logics. When I joined my first professional bureaucratic organization, I of course thought that decisions were the result of deliberate, planned processes based on rational calculations, studies, cost–benefit analysis, evaluations, and impact assessments. But I saw and learned that decisions were also based on traditions, identity, predetermined bureaucratic rules, and regulations, on what was regarded acceptable. I saw decisions based on imitation and copying, on timing, on the need to keep up, or on direct demands from external key players. In the Foreign Affairs sector, I saw many purely symbolic decisions linked only to the need to promote a picture of effectiveness, political or moral correctness, or social responsibility. And I have seen how money, corruption, and personal gains provide another complicated platform for why decisions are taken, a platform linked to a host of symbolic justifications for these decisions. On the other hand, I have also seen that *what is reasonable, sensible, appropriate, and rational to do is not just to take decisions that are based on the logic of technical rationality.* So many decisions made on logics of identity, networks, traditions, adaptations, imitation, power, and symbols might be fully reasonable and equally effective. Most decisions make sense when we first understand the specific logic used. And I have learned that I only understand that logic if I am located very close to the decision makers and the actual decision-making process. A decision will normally contain a mix of different logics and a good decision is normally the one that is based on a balanced assessment of the relative importance of the different logics. I have learned that the decision, however, always will and should be presented as if it was based solely on technical rationality.

Anchor 2: Know Your Sector

We have our own individual context, the people that surround us. Projects have their own specific context, the technical, people, power, and complex unforeseen issues that surround them. We work in organizations with their own specific organizational characteristics. And then this is all wrapped up in a sector context—a sector that anchors our professional efforts and impacts. We may change sectors over our career but not many times. Sectors are deep anchors of our profession and professionalism.

I have experienced that the few times I have encountered complicated or even wicked personal, project, or organizational contexts, I run. And correctly so. We shall remove ourselves from the people, projects, or organizations that create complications, unhappiness, or wickedness. We shall move on to other people, other projects, or other organizations. But I have also experienced that when I have encountered problematic sectors, I have realized this much too late, and often did not run but stayed too long. And when I ran from a sector, I left more unconsciously, more quietly, out the back door.

This is an opinion piece I published in *Politiken*, a leading Danish newspaper in 1996:

I have come to the city of Samara in Russia, where I have now been working for two years on an EU funded project. The project aims to train public top administrators and private business leaders in market economy and modern western public administration. Samara is a city of just over a million people located on the Volga River, 1,100 km southeast of Moscow. Samara is a city with proud traditions. The city is a center of knowledge and technology in Russia and has nine universities. This is where the Russian spaceship launches were conceived and this is where the Lada factories produce Lada cars for the whole of Russia, two per minute. Like many other Russian cities, Samara has been a closed city due to the city's military industry. It was only with Perestroika that people from Samara would be allowed to leave and that the doors were opened to foreigners. The first American to legally come to Samara arrived in 1992. In his wake followed many others: Mormons, Adventists, American Peace Corps, fortune hunters of all kinds, businessmen and administrators of about ten EU-funded projects, including mine.

I think everyone that has traveled or lived in Russia since the fall of the Berlin wall agrees that Russia does not leave one unmarked. For me the most striking thing has been that the place and the people here are so similar to where I come from. Take a walk in the countryside, go for a walk in the city or discuss with a hospital director, there is not that much that separates Samara from Denmark. Still, the extent of the material decay is truly depressing. The city center has not seen a craftsman in the last many decades, public areas are not maintained, the sewer system broken. Nothing has been done to beautify anything. The similarities all too clearly emphasize this unnecessary decay, that it did not have to be like this. That the decay is material not intellectual, I am constantly reminded of in my work which consists of teaching university lecturers and public sector top managers in Western management. Theoretically, there is not much I can teach them, the requirements for being a hospital director here does not differ much from being a hospital director in Denmark. The material and financial differences are obvious, but structurally and managerially it is all pretty much the same. The difficulty in working here is that I am often caught in the history between East and West. No matter how much I try to avoid it, a we-know-better or this-is-how-it-should-be-done easily come to the fore, for them and for me. How to talk about the Danish waste management, hospital, social and educational system without being caught in a Danish we-are-good and exposing their lost opportunities. This balancing act is almost impossible. That some western experts do not even try does not make it easier. I have met plenty of western advisers who do not think about balances, but immediately take the visible differences as a starting point and tell the hospital director at the first meeting that Russia is 30 years behind, what problems the hospital has and how they could be solved. It is depressing that experienced Russian managers find themselves exposed to such arrogance and ignorance.

What am I doing here? I am working and making a living. And I try to do it as professional and humble as possible. And that is not easy. There are so many barriers and contradictions to overcome: the language is a huge barrier, the defense mechanism are barriers. There are so many balances to keep: East, West, the obvious shortcomings of their system, the danger of not succumbing to stereotyping. Working as a western consultant in Russia these years is balancing on a knife edge, professionally and emotionally and has challenged my professional opinions, attitudes and values. I wonder if all these good Russian top managers also were challenged in their opinions, attitudes and values through their meeting with me?

My professional experience in Russia in 1996 for the first time exposed me to a complicated professional sector context and my article highlighted the dilemmas and my own muddling through. Being a young academic with six years of professional experience in the Danish municipal system teaching modern western management and administration to a group of elderly experienced Russian top managers in Samara, doom was written on the wall. But I, at the time, could not fully see this. I had just joined the international division of a large consultancy company. This was my first time working in Russia. I could sense something was wrong, but apart from knowing I was too young and inexperienced for these professionals, I was not fully able to grasp the depth of the political, cultural, historical, and conflictual contextual issues I, and the sector I was working in, was up against, and I think only my nervousness and humility to some degree carried me through. At least I completed the assignment and got my first deserved experiences with vodka in unlimited quantities.

Should I have accepted the position, should I have left earlier, should I have analyzed the sector context better? Exposure and knowledge sharing is normally always good, for me and for them, but sometimes the sector context puts us in such dilemmas that it is almost impossible to balance. I knew something was wrong in the us-teaching-you setup. And then I continued for many years in the foreign aid sector working in Asia and Africa, where the sector dilemmas, balances, and context not exactly became less complicated.

And if that was not enough, when I was in the foreign aid sector, I got thrown into the environmental sector, a sector with a host of other dilemmas—and not of my own planning. I was in the foreign aid sector when a strong Danish politician became the Minister of Environment and managed to pull with him a percentage of the foreign aid sector budget to the Ministry of Environment and, for a decade, launched a galaxy of Danish environmental projects and consultants onto the world before the budget again was transferred back to the Ministry of Foreign

Affairs. My decade in Asia in the environmental subsector of foreign aid was fully determined by this movement of budgets between ministries in Denmark. My two long-term projects in Asia were part of the galaxy of new environmental projects financed by the Danish Ministry of Environment. And I became engulfed in the problems and dilemmas of environmental issues and concerns stemming from popular activist movements in the rich world transferring to middle- and low-income countries with different agendas, priorities, and political contexts—and to the technical problems of making the nonsensical environmental impact assessment (EIA) system work in praxis.

My foreign aid and environmental sector platforms then secured me a position as development councilor at the Danish Embassy in South Africa, a position where many of the projects I managed were linked to the Danish focus on environmental development assistance, good governance, and anticorruption, all nonpriority sectors for the South African government. When I left the embassy and started out as an entrepreneur, I thought I finally had left these complicated often nonsensical sectors behind me—the deep dilemmas of the foreign aid sector and the bulldozing environmental movement. I now just had to concentrate on chasing and winning contracts, and then implement them professionally to the satisfaction of all involved. The sectors should be farming, construction, and energy, all national priority sectors. But my old sector platforms followed me. I won environmental consultancy projects as this was where I had many references. Then I started to dream up my own projects. I designed and got funding for projects that would support economic development for poor farmers, and these agro-village projects took me right back into development assistance and all the problems of this sector. Now it was not foreign aid, but projects that were anchored in the national development state, the national agricultural support industry. And it was all the same. The same problems and dilemmas of trying to help others from the outside. That these agro-projects were anchored in wicked contexts did not help. I should not have gotten involved in South Africa's own version of foreign aid, the development state. The agro-villages put me right back into all the problems I thought I had left behind. It never works when we want to be ambitious on behalf of others.

For my selection of the people, projects, and organizations that have surrounded me, I feel I have been not fully but somewhat in charge. My selection of the sectors I have spent most time in, in hindsight, looks more accidental, not fully, but my anchoring in these sectors still has the feel of me just following the flow and chances that passed my way. I have followed sector flows determined by the period, flows that at the time were invisible to me.

This unconscious sector anchoring is probably what annoys me most about my professional career. It annoys me that I got involved in the environmental sector without having chosen this sector; it annoys me it took so long to acknowledge that the aid sector, whether foreign or national as in South Africa through the development state, is fundamentally wrong; and it annoys me that it was so difficult for me to leave this sector. If I could tell the younger version of myself something, it would be to be careful of the invisible rising tides of sectors that pass by. Be careful of sector slipstreaming, as sectors rotate, become fashionable and unfashionable, and even irrelevant when the world rotates faster than the sectors.

Anchor 3: Know Your Globalization

At university, some of my professors were staunch Maoists and still today it makes me wonder how they could get it so wrong. I was 20, rural, and knew nothing, but they were 50 and professors! They are my go-to example of how wrong we can get it if we do not know the big picture we are part of, of how limited global information we had just few decades ago, and more importantly, of how poor professionals we become if our efforts are based in wrong mental models and big picture understandings. These professors became extremely poor professionals.

I have been pushed around the world for the last three decades. I have worked in Europe, Asia, Russia, and Africa. I have become global. And I have been part of mega-trend transitions and changes, some I knew I was part of, but some, honestly, not. It can be difficult to grasp these big picture mega-trends from our own small point of view. As backpacker, I visited China in 1991, just after China opened up to visitors, and I saw poverty and ignorance on a scale I had never seen before. To experience millions of people living in extreme poverty, to experience the ignorance that came from having been delinked for decades from everything but their own small backyard, is something I will never forget. I came back to China 30 years later and have never felt so proud of a place. To have pulled hundreds of millions out of poverty and rural ignorance and opened the country to the world was such an extraordinary achievement.

After 20 years submerged in foreign aid and environmental management projects, I read that some 650 million people had come out of poverty in the last decade and thought not only had I not fully realized this stunning and hugely impressive fact, but I did not also know the mechanisms and details of how it had happened. Here was clearly something I have missed in the decades where my attention had been swallowed in specialized development projects. I needed to read again, as the scale and newness to me pointed toward a need for updated mental models. What had happened did not look like the effects of the globalization I knew. One of the most disturbing aspects of the globalization I knew was its association with the poverty trap of the developing countries. Now 650 million people in developing countries had risen above the poverty line within a decade, a truly mind-boggling number at a truly mind-boggling speed.

When I missed the big picture, it felt almost embarrassing, but it has also been an important reminder. I have realized that, with the fast changes that happen all around, I need to commit serious time and energy to constantly upgrade my mental models, to re-educate myself. I must know and align my efforts to the real contextual big pictures to better my professional achievements. This is where the book *The Great Convergence* by Richard Baldwin comes in.[2] It provides a very valuable big picture mental model for our present new age of globalization and the impacts it has on us all.

Baldwin's main point is that globalization can be thought of as a progressive reversal of the forcible bundling of production and consumption and that three costs of distance matter: the cost of moving goods, the cost of moving ideas, and the cost of moving people. These three costs form three constraints that limit the separation of production and consumption, and their unbundling is the main driver for globalization. Understanding the evolving nature of globalization requires a sharp distinction among these three separation costs. The cost of moving all three things was very high before globalization began. These costs were constraints in the sense that all three forced consumption and production to be near each other. The costs or constraints were relaxed in order. The cost of moving goods came down first, followed by the cost of moving ideas. The third constraint, the cost of moving people, face-to-face interactions, remains costly and has yet to be relaxed. This simple entry point results in a fascinating new take on globalization, its causes, and impacts.

As the climate warmed and stabilized about 12,000 years ago, food production moved to people rather than people to food. The Agricultural Revolution meant that production and consumption were still bundled, but with the decisive difference that the production consumption bundles now were in fixed locations. Production was first localized with consumption in four river valleys that were in the crop-growing sweet zone about 30 degrees north of equator and subject to annual flooding that solved the bane of ancient farming—soil exhaustion. The presence of lots of people and food in the same four locations for thousands of years led to the rise of prosperous civilizations in Egypt, Mesopotamia, India, Pakistan, and China. The Asian centers of civilization were the economic focal points, and the global economy that emerged was dominated by these fixed locales of Asian clusters of bundled production and consumption. These clusters in Asia dominated the planet's economic activity and presided over world affairs in every sense of the word until the 14th century. Writing, cities, organized religion, government, laws, full-time armies, ethics, arithmetic, literature, poetry, and just about every other aspect of human society were invented in the production and consumption clusters to the east, south, and west of the Tibetan Plateau. Trade rose among all clusters but volumes were severely limited by high transport costs.

This dominance shifted when the constraints of distance were overthrown leading to the dominance of the North Atlantic countries from the 1820s. The steam revolution triggered a phase transition that eventually launched a new globalization stage and the first unbundling. It became economical to consume goods that had been made far away. Globalization in this phase meant the geographical unbundling of consumption and production on a massive scale. Mastery of intercontinental distances opened the door to interconnected trade, agglomeration, and innovation, which together turned the world economic order on its head. In one of history's most dramatic reversals of fortune, the Asian core became the periphery, and the North Atlantic periphery became the core. The civilizations in Asia and the Middle East were displaced in less than two centuries by a small group of countries in North Europe and North America. The outcome, *the Great Divergence,* explains how so much economic, political, cultural, and military power came to be concentrated in the hands of so few. This first globalization started around 1820 and was associated with the demographic transition and the rapid industrialization of the rich G7 countries of the United States, Germany, Japan, France, Britain, Canada, and Italy. This triggered a self-perpetuating spiral that produced an epic shift in the world economy. From 1820 to about 1990, the G7's share of global income soared from about 20 to 70 percent.

The growth in the G7 economies created income divergence, big time. Due to the magic of compound growth, even small growth-rate differences produce shockingly large differences over a few decades. Falling cost boosted trade, but moving goods did not make the world flat; quite the contrary. Manufacturing became even more concentrated to keep complex industrial processes working smoothly, and manufacturing processes became microclustered inside industrial zones located in the G7 countries. Productivity surged in the North, and this sparked a cycle of industrialization, agglomeration, and innovation that yielded the huge North–South knowledge gap, which in turn led to the unprecedented divergence of incomes. This was the globalization I knew all too well.

Since 1990, rapidly falling communication and coordination costs ended the second constraint, the cost of moving ideas. The spectacular fall in the price of computing power and the equally spectacular rise in fiber-optic transmission interacted to dramatically decrease communication costs. Today, it is almost costless to maintain a continuous, two-way flow of words, images, and data. For digitized ideas, distance truly died. By relaxing the constraints that had underpinned the vast imbalances in the global distribution of knowledge, the ICT revolution unleashed a historic transformation that created impacts of unprecedented complexity and speed. We are still in the very beginning of the second unbundling, and for most of us, it is still difficult to fully grasp its mind-boggling impacts. The second globalization is very different from the first globalization and is affecting professionals and everyone in radically new ways.

For millions of people, the second globalization has been a miracle-sized blessing. From a global perspective, it is hard to exaggerate how radical the effects have been.

The upward spiral for the G7 countries during the first globalization was reversed from 1990. For the last three decades, the G7 GDP share has fallen at a mighty pace and G7's world share is now back to where it was in 1914. The 170-year crash of India and China turned into a climb, and the two Asian giants' share of world GDP has risen sharply. At the base of these gigantic GDP changes was the evening out of the very uneven distribution of productive know-how that had emerged in the first globalization. This GDP share shift tells us that the nature of globalization changed radically around 1990. The shift is shown in the GDP share shift graph, which is an excellent mental model in all its simplicity (two factors only: years and GDP share, divided into three groups of countries, G7, I6, and rest of the world—RoW) and its ability to highlight key aspects of the world today. The shift, the *Great Convergence*, has been the dominant economic fact of the last three decades. It is the origin of much of the antiglobalization sentiment in the G7 countries and much of the new power and assertiveness of the new emerging Industrializing Six or I6 countries of China, South Korea, India, Poland, Indonesia, and Thailand.

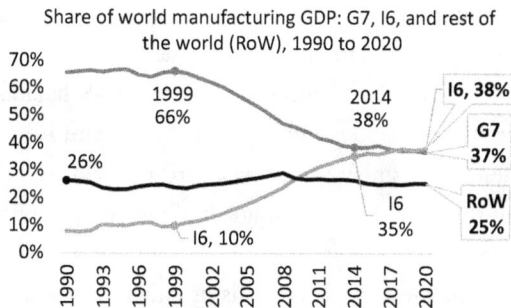

Share of world manufacturing GDP: G7, I6, and rest of the world (RoW), 1990 to 2020

I6 is China, India, Korea, Indonesia, Thailand, and Brazil
B7 is France, Italy, Germany, United Kingdom, Japan, United States, and Canada

The Second Globalization

The ICT revolution and the huge GDP share shift between G7 and I6 countries were accompanied by a dramatic changeover in global value chains and manufacturing. The G7 witnessed an accelerated decline of their share of world manufacturing to below 50 percent, a manufacturing share loss that showed up as share gains in very few countries, as only the I6 countries saw their share of world manufacturing explode. The manufacturing share of the RoW was largely unaffected by these changes. China's manufacturing sector, which was completely uncompetitive in 1970, rose rapidly from about 3 to 20 percent and is the largest manufacturer in the world today. The rapid industrialization of the I6 boosted their growth and considering that almost half of all people in the world live in these six countries, this growth explosion has had momentous ripple effects.

Relaxing the communications constraint, unfortunately, did not make the world flat. The G7's GDP share loss went to the few I6+ countries, which saw their global GDP shares rise by 30 percent. The internationalization of production created Factory Asia, Factory Europe, and Factory North America, not Factory World, and most international production networks and value chains today are regional, not global. The RoW, almost 200 countries, only had a GDP share rise of 3 percent. Developing countries outside the new global value chain-defined boundaries found it hard to push their combinations of low tech and low wages. The magic of the second globalization is not working in these countries, and the situation in these low-income countries has generally been untouched by the second unbundling. The revolutionary changes in economic growth, poverty reduction, and manufacturing in the second globalization have, for the most part, bypassed South America and sub-Saharan Africa. However, once wages get high enough in both the G7 and I6+ countries, the offshoring destinations may spread even further afield, and the geographical spread of the second unbundling could widen, likely first to the east coast of Africa.

If the cost of moving people falls as much as the cost of moving goods and ideas has in the past, we could be in for yet another radical global transformation. The driving force is simple. Despite the Great Convergence, salaries and wages are much higher in the rich countries, now theG7 plus the I6+ countries, and there are billions of professionals, project managers, engineers, designers, accountants, lawyers, publishers, and teachers in the RoW who would like to earn those wages. They are today unable to do so since they find it hard to get into the rich countries.

The next radical globalization change will involve professionals in one country undertaking production and service tasks in another, tasks that today require physical presence. The third unbundling would happen through technologies such as telepresence that would create very close substitutes to being there in person and could do to the service sector what the second unbundling did to the manufacturing sector. As almost two-thirds of all jobs are in the service sector, this impact will be dramatic and could provide a real opportunity for poor countries' professionals.

When we get our mental models right, we also get our facts right. The second globalization is a good fact-based mental model that helps us understand our professional context better. The mental model of the second globalization with its IT and global value chain revolutions provides us a platform to better understand big picture transitions and changes that happens all around us.

It helps us to understand which poverty reduction mechanism really works. In only a few decades, the second globalization took hundreds of millions of people out of poverty and released most of the world's poor from the first globalizations poverty trap. I will always be on the side of the global poor and this transformation was breathtaking in its scale. The second globalization in the last decades from the standpoint of the global poor, in particular the poor in China and India, has been a miracle. It is a fact, and it is only if we choose to take a standpoint from a select few or from local special interests that we can oppose the second globalization. For the second globalization to do its magic for the remaining 600 million global poor, it has to disperse to countries and areas not included in the first waves.

And it helps us understand and prepare for the new professional playing fields we can expect because of the unbundling mechanism and the global dispersion and agglomeration mechanisms. We will continue to see massive flows of G7 professionals and know-how from G7 to I6+ countries because the high-tech, low-wage combination turned out to be a world beater. We will see a massive capacity and skill upgrading for I6+ professionals. We will see billions of new Asian professionals enter the professional market in the coming decades. We will see the time of G7 professionals sitting tight on professional knowledge fast coming to an end. We will see more professionals become professional globalists and we will see ever more professionals move to and between the global-linked mega-cities located in Factory Asia, Factory Europe, and Factory North America. We will see an exponential increase in knowledge sharing, collaborations, and distributed networks between professionals in these regions. We will see professionals in one country undertake production and service tasks in another, tasks that today require physical presence. We will soon experience telepresence, and telerobotic provided an entirely new playing field for professionals. We will see professionals in rich countries in direct wage competition with poor countries' professionals providing their services remotely. And we will see a host of changes in professional work practices, as the ICT revolution will continue to make it easier, cheaper, faster, and safer to coordinate separate complex activities spatially.

I became a professional globalist in the second globalization, constantly pushed from location to location, from country to country, 24 to be precise. It has been estimated that, in 1900, around 1 percent of the world's population was globalists, working permanently in global positions, while today this number has grown to above 10 percent. I am a globalist 10 percenter. The second globalization sparked a massive flow of professionals and know-how from the rich countries to the new fast-growing countries, mainly China, India, Indonesia, Thailand, Malaysia, Vietnam, Poland, Brazil, Mexico, and Turkey. This meant that many professionals in the rich countries, including myself, went global. I moved from a rich country to work in two of the new fast-growing countries, Thailand and Malaysia, just like so many other professionals in the second globalization. And I, like many other professional globalists, moved to the new global-linked mega-cities. My last two permanent working locations, Bangkok and Johannesburg, have been in these new global mega-cities. The second globalization and the ICT revolution triggered a host of changes in professional work practices, management practices, and relationships among governments, companies, and organizations, and had a profound impact on how global professionals worked. Now I could sit in Borneo and compare international environmental laws and regulations with ease. Now I could be outposted from HQ for years to faraway places and keep daily contact with my bosses. All this gave me a deep appreciation of what anchors me. I realized that the most important things that have provided me with roots, friends, and colleagues, the things that have anchored me wherever I have worked, have been my profession, professionals, and my middle-classness. These anchors have refrained me from becoming a free-floating de-anchored global individual or professional.

Anchor 4: Know Your Demographics

The global demographic transition, and the turbulence it creates, is something almost invisible to us, but because of its importance and impacts we must develop a mental model for this transition. Otherwise, our professional efforts will remain out of context. And our demographic mental model needs to be sharp. And you cannot get a better sharpener that reading Paul Morland's *The Human Tide*.[3] The demographic transition exemplifies the power of really big numbers. It shows us when we really need to be able to leave our small I and We behind.

The truly extraordinary thing about the human demographic transition is that it is predictable and global. The global demographic transition, the human wave, will continue to take its course regardless of what we think or do; its history is about facts, numbers, and consequences rather that ideologies, ideas, or speculation. The demographic transition results in profound transformations of our professional context, both the global one and the one we are locally engulfed in; it results in the rise and fall of states, in wars and great shifts in economic power between countries and people; it results in an ever-faster speed of change and unpredictability. The human wave has made a vast and too often overlooked background for all of this. To leave demography out is to miss what may be the most important explanatory factor for the last 240 years and will continue to influence us all throughout this century.

Notestein described in 1911 what would be known as the demographic transition. A country would start with a high fertility rate, a high mortality rate, and a small population (stage one); then its mortality would fall, causing the population to grow rapidly (stage two); next, fertility would decline, resulting in continuing but slower growth (stages three and four); and finally, fertility and mortality would be back in balance, with the population stable again but at a much higher total population level (stage five). And he showed that each stage in the demographic transition will have a significant different population composition in relation to age groups. The demographic transition with its five different stages, each with its distinct age composition, significantly impacts a wide range of society and economic contexts. The demographic wave stirs things up and creates changes and critical turbulences. The demographic transition started around 1800, will end around 2100, and will result in an increase in the global population from 1 billion to around 10 billion. The demographic transition graph is among the most interesting, simplest, and best mental models I have encountered. Two factors (fertility and mortality) and two impacts (population growth and age composition) give us the demographic wave and its turbulences and maybe the most important societal law ever discovered. Plot any country or area in the world on the graph and we have the basis to make a wide range of predictions in relation to the turbulence created, imperialism, war, power shifts, crime, youth movements, and ethnic conflicts, you name it.

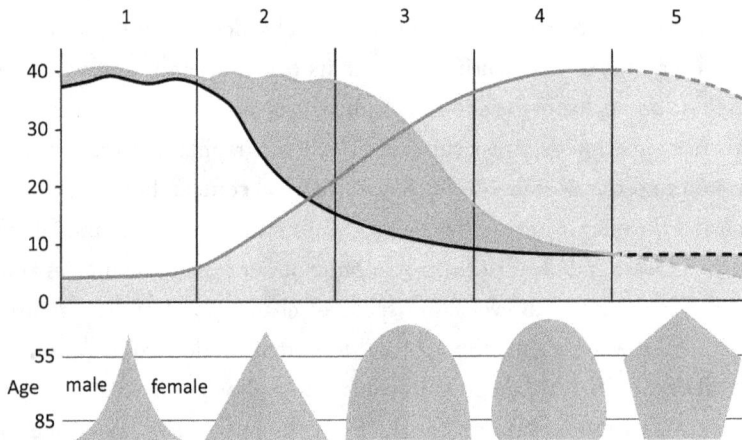

The demographic transition

The demographic transition is powered by a combination of the most basic means, the increased washing of hands, better water supply, rudimentary but critical interventions in pregnancy and childbirth, improved general health care, and diet. None of these would have been possible on a global scale without education, particularly of women, again often rudimentary but radically better than nothing, allowing life-preserving practices to be disseminated and practiced. The drop that starts the human wave is made up of a fall in early childhood mortality combined with general lower mortality rates in a country. When, after the mortality rate has dropped, the number of children born continues at the same rate, the number of people in a country explodes. The fall in mortality can cause a population to quadruple in a few decades with profound consequences for the economy, the ability to raise an army or send migrants overseas. As living conditions improve, people live longer; yet for a time, people continue to have large families of six or seven. Only later do family sizes decline. This delay brings along the population explosion. And this explosion brings along first youth bulges, then aging societies.

All countries and areas in the world go through this demographic transition, and the rapid population acceleration and deceleration in the demographic transition send shockwaves around the world wherever they occur. Once this immense speeding up and then quite sudden slowing down are apprehended, it is possible to get a sense of the huge impacts these demographic waves has had and will continue to have in this century.

When we understand the demographic transition, from its viewpoint of the many, it is so much easier to understand many of the things that currently happen around us, that happened in the past and will happen in the future. And it challenges so many of the not-so-deep opinions and mental models we might have developed without really having thought about it. It reminds us that nobody stays winners forever; that most of the turbulences we experience are not determined by cultural, religious, or whatever superfluous factors postulated but are part of demographic waves that hit all peoples, one region after another; and that imperialism, colonization, wars, shifts in economic powers, irrational youth movements, and ethnic conflicts are deeply linked to the ebbs and flow of the demographic transition, of the simple counting of how many people there are, of who increased their numbers first, and of age distribution. One factor with so many implications. One factor that when not realized and internalized make us talk nonsense. One factor that frames and impacts our professional life in so many ways, ways that depend on our age, birthplace, and where we undertake our professional work.

Much about demography is baked into the future and is certain to happen. We know that we will end up with a global population of around 10 billion. We know how many 50-year-olds will there be in Nigeria or

Norway, or anywhere for that matter, in 2060. We know that all countries will become countries where old people will dominate. We know that most professionals in the future will be mature professionals. Society after society is becoming older and, by the end of the century, most countries will have a median age over 50. Such aged societies have never been seen in history. We know that the demographic future will be less white and that most professionals in the future will be Asian professionals. We know that when the demographic wave comes to a stop, the world will become a more peaceful and law-abiding place as there is a strong correlation between demographic transition and its youth bulges, wars, violence, and crime. Not all young societies are embroiled in violence, crime, and war, but all old societies are at peace.

Demography makes a real difference, and past, present, and future events would not have been possible without the demographic wave. The general wave has created better lives for all. The turbulence in the different phases of the wave has, among many other things, created imperialism and colonization, wars, shifts in economic powers, and irrational youth movements.

The first population explosion allowed Britain and then more widely the people of Europe to dominate the globe. The demographic waves then played a major role in forcing their retreat. In Britain, the average yearly population growth was around 0.4 percent in the 1700s, historically normal. The British population growth then accelerated in the 1800s to exceed an annual 1.3 percent on average. When a population, or anything else, is growing 1.3 percent per annum, it doubles in around 50 years, then doubles again in the next 50 years, and that is what the population of Britain did during the 1800s. The fact that Britain's population was moving upward first and fast mattered. Numbers count. Without its population growth, Britain would not have become the leading imperialist. People were required to become imperialists and people were what Britain had in abundance. Imperialism has come and gone, likely never to reappear, as it was so closely linked to the first population growth explosions the demographic transition brought upon us.

For the first group of countries entering the demographic transition, the transition ignited wars. What first appeared an unbeatable and unique British demographic formula turned out to be only a bit of a head start. The British demographic explosion, which had given Britain the head start to colonize, spilled over to Germany and Russia in the early 1900s. Each of these waves created a population explosion and a youth bulge and these first three population waves of Britain, Germany, and Russia created in the first 50 years of the 1900s wars and destructions on a scale never seen before. What has been distinctly different between the first European population explosion and the later Asian population explosion in China, India, and South-East Asia has been the turbulence of war. Asia has during its demographic transition enjoyed the benefits of peace between countries. The focus for Asian countries has not been wars or national expansions but economic growth with impressive reductions in poverty levels. The consequences of having followed the European war and imperialist expansion paths, with populations of not hundreds of millions but billions, would have been unimaginably grim.

The European head start in the demographic transition led to hubris as it seemed to those who first came into the demographic transition that their advantage would last forever. They did not, and still do not, realize to what extent global dominance, whether imperial or economic, was built on foundations of early population expansion. China entered the demographic transition around 50 years later than the Europeans and China's population in the 1950s grew at nearly 3 percent, making China the first country to pass the one billion mark with a peak of 1.5 billion in 2030. Once the Asian countries started to combine size with industrial progress, just through the scale of their populations, China, India, and South-East Asia cannot fail to become major global political and economic entities. The demographic numbers in Asia will be driving world history and power in this century just as surely as they did when Europe entered the demographic transition.

It proved to be a curse when countries suddenly became flooded with young people. Wars, civil unrest, violence, and dangerous irrational youth movements, the demographic youth bulges of the last two centuries have given us it all. The devastating turbulence created by these youth bulges has been experienced in countries from Britain and Germany through Russia and China to the Middle East and sub-Saharan Africa today. The youth bulges in Europe in the first decades of the 1900s contributed to two destructive world wars. In China, the youth bulges in the 1960s and 1970s contributed to the complete collapse of the economy and irrational attacks on the elder generations. In China, it created the Red Guards and, in the West, the era of mass teenage or youth culture. This was confident and influential youth generations because they were large generations. In 1965, the under 25-year-olds represented half of the population in the United States; this has since fallen to under a third resulting in a general retreat of youth culture dominance.

Africa south of the Sahara is the final wave in the global demographic transition. Sub-Saharan Africa is today in the first stage of the global demographic transition, with exploding populations. Nigeria will go from 180 million people to massive 800 million by the end of the century. It is in sub-Saharan Africa that the different demographic turbulences of war, ethnic, and youth bulges are at their most intense. But these turbulences too will calm down. That we know.

But only if we read can we see these, as the demographic transition and its large-scale impacts and turbulence are hard to spot from our own small viewpoint. There were so many turbulences created by the demographic transition that I did not see when I was in the middle of it all. I did not see that my parents became victims of the youth bulge. They were rural, had little education, and were overwhelmed by the hordes of educated, confident, and outspoken youth in the 1970 and 1980s. In discussions and many other areas, they were outmaneuvered. Their life and working experience mattered little. I feel sorry for my father skillfully building and repairing houses with his own hands, quiet and mild spoken, but never given a chance to speak, to share his experiences and lessons learned. I often wondered how we could get to where we, professors and all, valued youth and inexperience higher than experience and professionalism—where reference points accumulated through lived life, where experience and maturity became so looked down upon. Now I know. It was the impact of these demographic turbulences, the youth bulge, that swept the world with different strength at different times and locations. But it is still painful to think about. It made my father's life so much less than it could have been. The turbulences of the demographic youth bulge still sweep across many countries. I experience it first-hand here in youthful South Africa, where there is too much radicalism, where discussions, politics, and plans become immature. To mindlessly discuss if mining or agriculture should be nationalized when that strategy has failed so many times. With experience, the discussion of ideologies becomes tiresome, while the how-to becomes the only interesting thing to discuss.

I thought I would never again see this youthful bullying, but here it is again, right in front of me. All youth bulges in the demographic transition, in all countries and everywhere, will pass but they take some tough decades to get through.

I professionalized in a period where most professionals were white and from the rich countries. I grew up under the influence of the winners as it is they that tell the story. I have had to work hard to become a global professional and to rid me of the hubris created by the white European head start in the demographic transition. The demographic transition reminds us that nobody stays winners forever. The billions of Asian professionals will change the winning field in this century. I want to slipstream, not fight, this demographic transition. Today, I know my demographics better and this has made my mental models sharper, made me fight my biases better, and made me a more rounded professional.

Anchor 5: Know Your Evolution

My decade as an entrepreneur has been hectic, and from the outside it might look like my 52 project wins have been all over the show with little strategic direction. From the inside, that is also how it has felt many times. But that does not mean there have been no patterns. The patterns, in hindsight, have been about a constant search for variation, differentiation, and specialization within the broad initial goals I had set and the initial conditions and general experiences I had in my baggage. The paths of my wins have been varied, some became one-timers, some repeatable, and some guided me in a certain direction. I have constantly sought areas where I could differentiate my offerings from others and in these differentiations, I have tried to specialize. Some differentiations went nowhere, and some provided a platform for further specialization. In hindsight, my entrepreneurial path has looked like having come straight out of Darwin's book. What I have learnt, not only as an entrepreneur, but in general as a professional project manager, is that throughout we must *evolve, differentiate, and cooperate*.[4]

Entrepreneurial, and professional, life is deeply rooted in nonlinearity and complexity, and we should not be surprised that our path is so uneven and unpredictable. Complex systems come together from the bottom up. They emerge. They evolve. They are not planned. They happen.[5] I, for sure, have experienced the emergent and complex nature and context of my entrepreneurial life. But I have also experienced that if I can spot emergence, I do have a head start and must slipstream on the emergent trend I have spotted. It is better to observe the context, for an entrepreneur the market, than to plan it. It is better to identify emergent trends and go with their flow. The ability to spot patterns and to know that patterns cannot be transferred directly from other contexts or markets, even if they are adjacent or appear similar, are important. In complex systems, we must be flexible and we must have not just one strategy but many and we must allocate some of our resources to long-odds bets and to experiments that will probably come to nothing but could contain the seeds of success.

Evolution requires variation, rejection of inferior or less well-received variants, multiplication of successful variants, and a commitment to further cycles of experimentation, variation, selection, and multiplication of the few winners. We must always accept the verdict of our external context, even when we consider it unfair. We must not give failing projects the benefit of doubt, and of all our opportunities and efforts, we should only expect to have a few winners, but those few winners provide platforms we need to get the most out of. We must accept failures and get on with working out what to do next.[6]

And what we should do next is slipstream. The process of differentiation means that if the wider context or market proclaims a new initiative a success, slipstream. Get on the bandwagon as fast and as far as possible. This means reproduction and new generations of improved versions of whatever are successful. And it means we should take the winning idea or project as far afield geographically as we possibly can as long as it will be a winner in the new context. It means adapting the winners to local context. Darwin's concept of niches means that there is an amazingly large number of ways to make a living and that the ideal position is to have our own niche where few others operate.

And Darwin's concept of *cooperation* gives us a good idea of how we must act to survive.[7] Business, and professional life in general, is driven by both cooperation and competition. Cooperation and competition are necessary complements. Competition becomes important when it forces itself on us. But cooperation is the more basic process. Without cooperation, we cannot do or produce anything. Deciding which professionals to cooperate with is therefore more basic and important than deciding which businesses or professionals to compete against. Competition takes care of itself, while cooperation requires a prior act of will. The professionals that win are those who cooperate best and have the best reciprocal cooperators.

Trust is the glue that keeps it all together. Beyond all professional transactions and developments lie trust. The way to get ahead is to have a large network of professional trustworthy cooperators. I am a cooperator and I, like all other cooperators, find it hard to deal with transparently self-interested people. To become successful, we need to network, cooperate, and build relationships with the professionals who possess cooperative attributes that can take us forward. This results in a number of musts for entrepreneurs and professionals: We must build a reputation as someone who creates reputation, skills, platforms, and wealth for others, and is trustworthy; we must always cooperate in the first instance; we must trust others until they prove themselves unworthy of trust; we must be willing to take turns in extracting advantage; we must appreciate that reciprocity is a long-term concept, not one requiring mutual advantage in each individual transaction. We must value that cooperation is cumulative and self-reinforcing, and we must seize all available opportunities to cooperate with useful professionals.

Project Story 3: From Project Manager to Project Developer in South Africa—Evolve, Differentiate, Cooperate

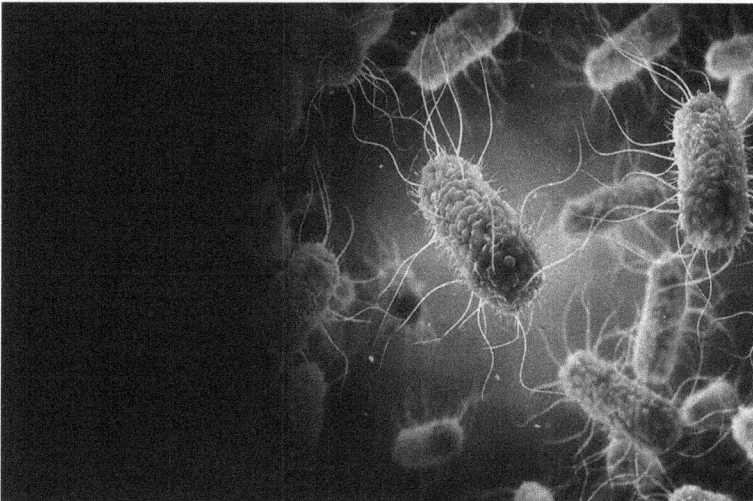

Microorganisms producing gas

After my last salaried job as a diplomat, I started out as an entrepreneur. Each career transition or change of career platform is challenging but having been able to become a sustainable entrepreneur in South Africa has been my toughest and maybe best career achievement. To jump from a professional good-salaried job to the uncertainties of being an entrepreneur is hard. The shift represents a deep contextual shift. I have seen many fail in the jump from public or salaried to private and entrepreneurial. Some think their network is so good that they can rely on their old contacts and colleagues for contracts to sustain a private business career. They are normally wrong and the walk back is tough. Of the 52 projects I have won since I started out on my own, only few came through people I knew from before.

Entrepreneurial Life

Being an entrepreneur is complex, but also very simple. When we have started out on our own, there is only one thing that matters. It is to get someone to sign on a piece of paper, a contract, that they will hand over money they are in control of to you. This transaction is the simplest thing in the world, but for an entrepreneur the most important and difficult of all. The pressure to win tenders or assignments starts from day one and continues throughout the entrepreneurial professional career. And it is all about the same thing, a signed contract, a financial closure. This simplicity can be difficult to grasp or accept when we come from other sectors, where many different agendas have equal importance. Working in a political office or an embassy or a health department, the demands, priorities, and mandates are multiple and overlapping. Not so being an entrepreneur, where the ability to get contracts at the end of the day overrides all other agendas or priorities. To win contracts, again and again, all our technical, people, political, and emergent slipstreaming skills must be present, and all on a high professional capacity level. Otherwise, we will not make it. Politicians that go entrepreneurial normally fail. They are good at political gaming, and that can be complex, but it is still only one of four required skills. Their technical (often absent) or people skills (often arrogant) may be lacking and then it is difficult to repeatedly win in the entrepreneurial game.

Why should anyone give us money by signing a contract with our name on. There are three basics that at least get us in contention—and without these, out of contention. In general, nobody will give us a contract if we have not done it before, if we have no competent professionals to do the job, or if our company is so small or financially weak that we could be gone by tomorrow. The absence of any or all these three would make the one with the money to be handed over nervous. Expressed in positive terms, it means we need to have a verifiable and specialized track record in the relevant field, have a team of competent professionals that can do the job here and now, and have scale and financial stability (the bigger the better). I have these requirements on my backbone as I have both been handing out and been applying for contracts for decades. I was an experienced proposal writer before I started as an entrepreneur, one of the reasons I have won relatively many tenders.

Besides these three basics, I have found that I cannot be an entrepreneur if I do not have a story to tell. A story I can tell with enthusiasm quickly, short, and to the point. A story that engages. I cannot be a salesperson for a thing, an energy-efficient pump or a solar panel, but that is just me. I must wrap my entrepreneurship into meanings and stories. My stories have been stories linked to innovations, poverty reduction, and rural and green developments in present-day South Africa. If it is not new, I cannot do it. If it does not have potential positive societal impact, I cannot do it. Again, that is just me. No moral lesson there.

The contracts won over the last decade have come from a wide range of international and national organizations: UNDP, USAID, GiZ, DBSA, IDC, Ministries of Energy, Environment, Rural Development, Trade and Industry and Science and Technology, and Johannesburg, Ekurhuleni and Tshwane municipalities. And they have covered a wide range of technical areas from renewable energy, energy efficiency, electricity, water, construction, biogas, bio-CNG, integrated rural and renewable energy, independent power producers (IPPs), public–private cooperation (PPP), green building technologies, wastewater, solid waste, carbon emissions, environment, transaction advisory, monitoring, evaluation, impact assessment to national policies and technical guidelines and manuals. It has been a whirlwind.

The first three years were dominated by consultancy and more consultancy contracts, for which my CV was strong, and I nearly collapsed.

Deadline upon deadline. It slowly dawned on me that even though this professional consultancy work was sufficiently profitable, it was physically unsustainable, and, in some ways, the hours put in also did not provide the returns I was aiming at or dreaming of. If we sell hours, there are only so many hours in a day to sell. I came to realize I had to change strategy and plan with a longer time span.

Working and living in South Africa, I started to look around at wealth and income creation in the different sectors I increasingly got involved in energy, construction, and farming. All these sectors have a three-ladder income and wealth structure. At the first ladder, we sell our time, per hours, days, or months, through our job or through consultancies. I spent my first entrepreneurial years exclusively on this ladder. At the second ladder, we gain income through project management, winning projects, implementing them, and then handing them over to the owners. We chase tenders and contracts, and when we win, we are good for a while until the project is completed and we must hustle and chase again. The size of the projects won and managed determine our wealth and income on this ladder, and even though the chasing and winning has a touch of lottery, at least the chance is there to get more wealth and become better off than the hourly fee-based income at the first ladder. From year three onward, I mainly worked on this ladder and consciously phased out most work on the first. I am still on this second ladder, which provides me with all my income and wealth. I still chase tenders and projects and still win some.

But from around year six, I began to dream of entering the last ladder: the asset and ownership ladder, where it is ownership and operation of assets that generate wealth. The owners of buildings, farms, power stations, retail, these are the professionals operating on the third ladder and here is a chance to make it even bigger. I wanted to move slowly from project management to project development, from project manager to project developer and owner of the asset.

When I began as an entrepreneur, I had a tiny start capital of 20,000 USD and being new in the market and country, I knew I had to climb the ladders by my own strength and resources, meaning winning and successfully implementing enough consultancy projects to create a financial platform to enter the project management area, where capital is required for successfully winning and implementing capital-based project. Within project management, I knew that scale is key, and I set targets for winning ever larger projects to create platforms in competence, capital, and experience to gain access to the next platform. Such scaled development would take me forward without stretching my resources or competences. For the first two ladders, I counted on winning grant-funded consultancy and project management contracts, which I then hoped would take me to loan and equity-funded own projects on the last ladder. I expected the first ladders to last seven years before beginning to overlap with my own funded projects. It took longer.

It took longer because I did not climb the ladder in a straight line. I knew I had to take the opportunities and chances that came my way. Any platform life brings us, we must use and optimize. Pragmatism rules. I also knew that progress is evolutionary. Planned or not, what came to happen was a step-by-step climb. And the steps were clearly linked to contract size. I grouped my contracts into five sizes: those below 0.5, 1, 5, 10, and 20 million USD. I am not sure where these size barriers came from, but I experienced them. There was a qualitative shift between each size level, both in relation to the difficulty in winning contracts on the next level and in the competence required to implement professionally on each contract size level. I experienced that when I had won and implemented three to five projects below one million USD, I had a better chance to enter the next level: below five million USD. I therefore started to aim for three to five projects won at one level and then, from this platform, send feelers or balloons (project proposals) up to the next level. When the balloon popped, I had entered the next level or platform. Accumulation of projects of a certain size gave me a platform, which I knew I had to take advantage of to the fullest. These simple numbers gave me guidance. And it taught me that it is very difficult to skip levels. Almost all who try fail or look silly, talking of a potential 10 million USD project, when the experience base is two 0.1 million USD projects. Number sense rules. The way of business is slow and evolutionary, and this shall impact and inform our thinking and talking. When we hear of people skipping levels, luck, an influential family, corruption, or something else is normally at play, and that does not guide us much.

After the exhausting consultancy years, I prepared a five-year strategy, probably the first and only career strategy in my life. The strategy included three priority sectors: energy, building, and farming, based on a recognition of the South African context, needs, and development opportunities mixed with my own interests. Being an entrepreneurial company with global experience, I wanted to bring new concepts to the South African market, not being one among many with the same skills and capacity. I zoomed in on international concepts guiding my five-year strategy, concepts centered around integrating rural economic development with renewable energy and introducing South Africa to biogas production and alternative building technologies.

And I put up balloons, and, to my luck, I had some pop in all three areas on contract-size level four. I suddenly had three emerging platforms for entering the third ladder.

Within the building sector, I won a couple of large construction projects, but found that the construction sector was filled with large, experienced construction companies which I could not compete with. I knew I had to specialize and entered a partnership with a Danish specialized alternative building technology company. We tested, certified, fine-tuned, and localized the technology into two of my projects and managed to build 70 houses with the alternative building technology. But the high-performance, high-strength concrete technology we used was not suitable to be transferred and localized. It was heavy and clumsy and could not compete with bricks and mortar. The market was not ready, and we were too inexperienced. We failed and I left the construction platform behind.

Within the farming sector, I also won two large agro-village projects. I had developed and adjusted an agro-village concept based on a century of experience with these concepts in Denmark. My concept was innovative, new for the country, and specialized, and provided me with a niche that looked promising for taking me to the third ladder. The concept received enthusiastic support and funding from the government. I constructed and handed over two agro-villages to the small-scale farmers. I started to plan the next agro-villages which I would finance and sell on the private market. Then the villages ran into serious operation problems: theft, in-fights, and so on took over and the villages collapsed. And I lost my platform for private funding and roll-out. I too realized very late that my growth strategy was reliant on other people's operation skills. I left the farming platform of the farming sector behind.

After my first seven entrepreneurial years, I had managed to develop a foothold in all my three priority sectors, but only one continued to look promising, so I went full stream for energy in the hope that, in this sector, I could get to the third ladder. I had a deeper experience base in the energy sector, as I, for long, had undertaken energy assignment for many clients: renewable energy policies, REFIT policies, national localization strategies, comparative fee analysis, municipal business plans, implementation of PV solar plants, LED lights, and solar water heaters. Especially the construction of two biogas facilities provided a promising platform for the last ladder. But how did I get from these won energy contracts on level two to ownership and assets? And what was my plan to be good and lucky enough to get there?

My idea of ownership had been the traditional one. Get funding, build something, own and operate it, and live off the profit until I die or pass it on to my family. That was how I had foreseen my stay at the third ladder. Then I met an old university friend, J.P. Vittrup, who worked in a department for innovation in Copenhagen. He told me something that had passed my attention. His department supported emerging entrepreneurial companies, and he said that the last decade had seen a dramatic change in how these new companies planned and strategized. And it was seen in all sectors from energy, bakeries, retail, coffee shops, manufacturing, IT, to gaming. The approach was built around unit modularity, standardization, scaling, and planned exit. Get the first bakery established, make it a success, then replicate it to five more locations, establish a combined three-year balance sheet worth looking at, and then sell off. I had seen entrepreneurial owner companies struggle with exit strategies when the owner got old or tired. Here the exit strategy was built in from day one. I liked what I heard. It was an approach that was perfectly tuned to the IPP power purchase agreement (PPA) energy sector. Develop a renewable energy facility, standardize size and technology, scale up, operate, and sell off the special-purpose vehicle (SPV) companies with not only a balance sheet but with a signed 20-year PPA. Selling future guaranteed turnover. A clear exit strategy. I was in. But I knew it would be difficult to take me there. The IPP field is mainly for the big players. I wanted to be on my own and had to find my own path to become an IPP on the third ladder.

My Biogas Idea and Its Context

I was in awe. I was visiting a Danish biogas plant with my partner Peet Steyn. It was the first time I saw a large-scale biogas plant and a five-megawatt generator. The scale of this single unit generator, the noise, the vibrations, the power. And it was run solely by tiny microorganisms, eating and letting the air go. No chemicals, no additions, just organic waste being eaten by these microorganisms in huge tanks and then the gas being collected to run this monster generator. It was magic happening right there in front of me. I was sold. And I decided that I wanted to introduce this magic to South Africa. Peet had already made up his mind. He is an engineer. They plan.

I had spare time and resources to chase my dream of becoming an IPP. I knew it would take time. I had patience and no panic. And I knew from my previous entrepreneurial experience in South Africa what I wanted. I wanted a project that was not dependent on grants or on government. I wanted simplicity in the context, no communities, no politicians, no wickedness. I wanted a pure private sector project, private input suppliers and private buyers, funded by normal lenders and equity funders on normal conditions. I wanted only technical and financial experts around me. I wanted to become an IPP expert in biogas project development. And I wanted scale and a clear exit strategy.

I had been involved in the South African IPP program from the beginning through my position at the embassy. I had seen the sector take off. I knew there was space in the renewable energy IPP sector, but also that I had to *differentiate and specialize*. There were four renewable energy sources available: wind, solar, biomass, and biogas. Biomass was found only in areas far away from where I stayed. Solar quickly saw an influx of suppliers; the technology is simple, imported, and quickly became a simple issue of price. Wind is only for the big players, as projects take a lot of money to develop and work best with scale; why, they quickly move into the billions. Out of my scale. Left was biogas: complicated to develop and operate but few developers and the sources close to where I stay. Unsexy but magical. I chose biogas.

I established a specialized biogas company EBF GAS with Peet. Peet had already built two biogas plants and we together built two more through linkages to some of my other projects. That gave us four bio-gas EPC (Engineering, Procurement, and Construction) on our resume, making us one of the biggest biogas EPC companies in the country (it was a small sector!). We visited biogas plants in Denmark and China. We visited equipment suppliers in China and Europa, we visited European biogas companies with decades of IPP experience. We studied and researched. We googled and read. We discussed technical and financial issues with potential feedstock suppliers, funders, and gas buyers. And then we differentiated and specialized further.

Within biogas, we had several choices, biogas to electricity, CNG (compressed natural gas), LNG (liquified natural gas), CHP (combined heat and power), and so on. We ended up with bio-CNG to differentiate our offerings from other participants in the biogas market and specialize within that biogas subsector. Then we had to specialize within the value chain of feedstock inputs, transportation, production, marketing, and sales, and we chose to specialize in bio-CNG production and cooperate with others to let them manage the other steps in the value chain. And then we had to optimize my production part of the value chain. We had to get the costs right. The IPP bio-CNG business is cutthroat as the selling price must be below competing energy sources. The main cost drivers are capital and feedstock costs. For feedstock costs, there is some variability but not much. Farmers know their stuff. So, to be able to make a viable business, we had to look carefully at technology supply and costs and quickly realized that technology suppliers from the northern countries pricewise would not work in the nonsubsidized South African context, and so we had to *look East*. We screened the supplier market. Alibaba has made a huge contribution to transparency. We got quotes from many different Chinese companies, visited the best several times, liked what we saw (decades of experience and proven track records, capable technical engineers and chemists, and scale), partnered with a Chinese company— one of the world's largest bio-digester and CNG manufacturers—and Capex costs fell to a level where we again had a viable IPP business.

Based on our experience from having undertaken 21 biogas feasibility studies, constructed 4 biogas facilities, and our visit to and discussions with international and national stakeholders, we found three potential strategic areas. The first area involved the development of smaller biogas facilities with on-site electricity production and consumption, a feed-stock of around six tons per day, and an investment cost of around half a million USD. The second area involved the development of large-scale CHP facilities with electricity and heat for industrial customers' own use, while the third area was development of large-scale bio-CNG (biological produced CNG) facilities with CNG gas for transport or industrial cus-tomers, feedstock in the last two cases around 175 tons per day, and an investment cost of around eight million USD. We decided to focus on the third strategic opportunity, the large-scale CNG facilities, and we decided to focus on own developed and owned facilities. We found that the CHP market would mainly be an EPC market and we wanted to move away from EPC contracts. We decided that our end goal was to develop, fund, construct, own, and operate five 200,000 GJ bio-CNG facilities. That would bring us the third ladder.

Then we put all this, the final idea based on multiple differentiations and selections, into context to be sure we had it right. I prepared a bio-CNG context report for nobody but us. We knew we had to be sure that our end goal made contextual sense in relation to the market, custom-ers, competitors, existing volumes, and suppliers. We had to be sure that the numbers made sense. Were we aiming too big? Too small? Does the market have space for one million GJ bio-CNG? What we wanted was a small but profitable platform in a niche market. We wanted to be a big player in a small pond. We did not want to enter a saturated market, or a sunset market for that matter, or be run over by competitors, new tech-nologies, or new natural gas sources. I prepared our contextual analysis to answer these questions. The method I used was the tried and tested: Goo-gle search, discussions with players in the field, and drawing and writing down my own conclusions.

The context analysis showed a small but growing CNG *market* in the country. And it showed that our planned quantities would fit well with our output amounting to half a percentage of the total natural gas consumption, but 15 percent of the CNG consumption in the coun-try, our bio-CNG furthermore being the first green CNG in the market. The analysis showed that there was a bio-CNG niche market in stand-alone production facilities linked directly to dedicated industrial or green fuel transport customers or through links to the existing CNG supply networks in cooperation with existing CNG gas traders, and that we would not get run over by a sudden influx of new or cheaper sources of natural gas as no new natural gas was expected to enter the market in the coming decade. Our feasibility studies had shown that we could produce bio-CNG to the market at a *price* of around 10 USD per GJ, lower than LNG, LPG (liquified petroleum gas), petrol, diesel, and paraffin but higher than natural gas, CNG based on pipeline gas and energy based on coal providing us with a tricky pricing context. The analysis showed that the *production of biogas* in South Africa was at a very early stage with only 16 biogas facilities installed with a combined capacity of around 15 MW and only 10 small biogas companies involved. Many of the biogas facilities had experienced operational issues, several had stopped production, and difficulties had been experienced with multisource feedstock-supplied biogas facilities. The many failures were a concern as funders do not like to fund upstart problems and failures. Our cooperation with a world-renowned bio-CNG manufacturer meant *technologywise* we would be fine, but as there were no operating bio-CNG facilities in South Africa, we knew we would experience resistance from funders as they prefer to see operating and functioning technology proven in the local context. The context analysis finally showed that the key constraint was the *access to feedstock*. Without feedstock in large, secured quantities, there is no bio-CNG facility, simple as that. We knew the annual tonnage required for a 200,000 GJ facility would be 50,000 to 80,000 tons depending on the organic source. This is serious quantity. We furthermore needed locations with single-source suppliers with bio-CNG offtakers not more than 150 km from the production site and with the production not more than 10 km from the feedstock source. Our analysis found that only cattle manure, chicken dung, and maize straw as feedstock could deal with these constraints and, based on a detailed study of potential suppliers and their locations, we concluded that 71 viable large-scale 200,000 GJ bio-CNG facilities could be established in South Africa, smaller than expected but clearly enough for our plan to establish five facilities.

To get a biogas project funded by the private sector, I knew we had to be thorough and cover all aspects of input, technology, and outputs. I knew we had to provide proper technical documentation. So, I converted our context analysis into a proper report, a market report, and developed two projects from scratch with full technical and financial descriptions and all supporting documents, which, for each project, came to more than 30 technical documents. We had beautiful PowerPoint presentations. And we were ready to take it all to the funders. Before I get to how that went, let me, for background, present how we put the idea into a strategy and a project.

The Idea Framed in a Strategy Concretized Into a Project

Based on the context analysis, we developed and wrote down our strategy—a strategy that showed our experience in the sector, had six main components, and showed our grasp of the key platforms of input, technology, and outputs; a strategy that would look convincing to funders.

Our strategy highlighted that we had been intensively involved in the biogas sector in South Africa during the last decade and had gained valuable experience in the feasibility, design, construction, and operation of biogas facilities. We had designed and constructed four biogas facilities and undertaken 21 feasibility studies. Through this, we had slowly and methodologically gained relevant context-specific local experience to undertake and implement new sustainable biogas developments. Our growth strategy involved the IPP establishment of five large-scale bio-CNG facilities in the Free State and North West Provinces. We found that bio-CNG as a commodity provided substantial better internal rate of return (IRR) than other outputs and would focus on closed-circle local systems of feedstock supply, production, distribution, offtake, and use of the bio-CNG produced to protect and delink production, use, and pricing as much as possible from external energy pricing and supply variations. We would develop facilities with one feedstock supplier, one offtaker, and one industrial end user. And we would not speculate in unproven income streams from liquid organic fertilizer or carbon trade. We had developed a close and fruitful development cooperation with one of the largest CNG traders in South Africa, and they would provide 20 years bio-CNG offtake for all our projects. We had had detailed discussions with large-scale potential feedstock supply farmers and we had formulated 10 detailed criteria for bio-CNG locations and feedstock supply and had made an initial selection of three preferred feedstock suppliers.

We would utilize only proven biogas and CNG technologies and had opted to utilize an adapted European technology design with cost-cutting imports from Asia to provide sustainable and profitable bio-CNG business cases. No technological first comer, no innovations, no breakthrough technologies were to be introduced. One of the world's leading biogas developers and biogas equipment manufacturer would provide the biogas and CNG technology and we would provide EPC services.

Those were the main ingredients in our bio-CNG strategy, and these ingredients were then applied to our project developments, the first being the Mushlendow bio-CNG facility. This project development would show if we had gotten our context and strategy right and if it was possible for us to develop a detailed specific bio-CNG project that was financially and technically viable.

The Project Information Memorandum (PIM) we developed for the Mushlendow project contained all key information as required by funders. We had completed the technical designs and financial modeling, land, feedstock supply agreement, CNG and fertilizer offtake agreement, and all permits, and the project was ready for implementation with a sustainable and profitable business case. The PIM showed that the project would make good money for all involved. We had a project with yearly bio-CNG sales of four million USD, Capex eight million, Opex two million, which gave us a project with a good 10-year IRR of 21 percent and a payback period off our years. We had, in the development, emphasized the correct location and balancing of the three main biogas components (inputs, processing, and outputs) to achieve a South African local-anchored long-term sustainable bio-CNG project. We had spent years to develop the strategy and the PIM and get the project ready for funding. The project was viable and ready to go. Or so I thought.

Postevaluation

When I started out, there was one biogas project in South Africa of the same size as the one we planned. It took that entrepreneur nine years to get started. Seven years to get to financial close, then two years to build. Seven years of project development, spending so much time and money with no return. First, I thought that cannot be true; something must have gone wrong. Then, that was poor. But it was true, and it was not poor. IPP project developments take time, and it will be frustrating. I have now used four years on the development of the Mushlendow project, spent time and money on travel, design, and permits, and I think we will start construction next year. But who knows? Something always happens. Why does it take so long? Why is IPP project development so complicated and difficult? What have I learnt from being an entrepreneur that attempts to go from project management to project development?

I learned that I had to fine-tune my project management skills. For a consultant or project manager, the project cycle management skills are at the forefront: the ability to go full project cycle from screening, proposal, contract management, implementation, to monitoring and evaluation. Project development with the aim to own is quite another matter. It revolves around four elements: *inputs, technology, and outputs, framed by funding.* Simple but complex. Each element has its own complications, and the sequence is not straightforward. I had to fine-tune my project management skills to be able to build viable input, technology, output, and funding platforms.

I learned that my technology skills did not have sufficient depth. I have technical and technology experience and skills but I had to admit that the chemical field of biogas production was well above my technical abilities. The biogas methane production process with four stages of hydrolysis, acidogenesis, acetogenesis, and methanogenesis, which are catalyzed by different specialized microorganisms, made my head spin. Ask me to optimize the production by tweaking feedstock type, pH, temperature, or other physical parameters to benefit microbial growth and biogas outputs and my metamemory quickly tells me that I need assistance. The need for a strong technical partner was obvious. Enter Peet Steyn.

I learned project finance is something else. Project finance is getting an idea financed. Without security. And that is of course difficult. I came from management of projects financed by others, and never had to finance a project of my own from external sources. I have never had a bank overdraft facility. I do not like banks. Now I had to raise money. To be exact, 10 million USD for the Koster project alone from a banking and funding sector I had never worked with. I went to my bank I had

had through the last decade and had one of my shortest meetings ever. They asked for three years operational and financial data. I said it was a greenfield project of which there was no similar in the country but many abroad, and I would (and could) not finance it from my balance sheet or from my private assets. End of that meeting. I had to learn quickly. They do corporate loan financing, I needed project finance—two very different things. I had to get new friends in a sector where my knowledge was shallow and where I had no network to speak of. Enter Motheo Tsatsi and Hope Segone, two qualified young finance professionals.

Project finance is the long-term financing of infrastructure and industrial projects based on the projected cash flows of the project rather than the balance sheets of its sponsors. Usually, a project financing structure involves several equity investors, or sponsors, and a group of banks or other lending institutions that provide loans to the project, normally non-recourse loans that are secured by the project assets, including the revenue-producing contracts, and repaid entirely from project cash flow, rather than from the general assets or credit worthiness of the project sponsor, me! Project lenders are given alien on all assets and can assume control of the project if the project company has difficulties complying with the loan terms. A special-purpose entity, an SPV, is created for each project, thereby shielding other assets owned by the project sponsor from the detrimental effects of a project failure. The SPV project company has no objectives and assets other than the project. Capital contribution commitments by the project sponsors, the owners, of the project company are necessary to assure the lenders' commitment. It is often said that project finance is more complicated than other financing methods. I can verify that.

So, to get the project financed, I had to find a group of equity and loan funders that would support me with 10 million USD. This depended to a high degree on the quality of the idea and the quality of the contracts and documents I could come with. And on the trust that could be established. The equity funders pull the train. Without equity provided as cash, no lender. These deals are normally structured with the loan-to-value ratio limited to 60 percent and therefore requires 40 percent equity contribution.

We started doing the rounds to the equity funders in town; Motheo knew many. These meetings were an eye opener. Even though I am not an engineer, I had worked with engineers for decades, and knew if I had a good, respected engineer by my side, I could enter anywhere. Or so I thought. Not the equity world. These guys talked a language neither me nor Peet could follow. It was LTV, DCF, DSCR, IRR in a constant flow. Project finance is such a specialized field that has developed its own language completely. Foreign to us. Practice, repetition, meetings, Motheo, and slowly we got traction with some of them. Trust started to develop.

It was clear that without me putting in cash, skin in the game as they say, it would be impossible. I allocated half a million USD of my own, which made me a partner that was willing to take risks for my own money. That would give me a 20 percent share in the SPV company we would establish for the Koster project. Equity funders are not playing. Cash in equals shares out. Clear and simple. This at least made the equity structuring easier. I might be able to get a 2 percent project development fee for my efforts at financial close, but this was not what I was interested in. I am a project man. I want to see and participate in projects on the ground.

With equity commitments on board, I could move on to lenders. I thought, coming through with equity support letters from reputable equity funders and myself in place, we were almost there. I was wrong. I now knew that traditional banks were out, which left only the international and national development financing institutions as possible lenders. I knew some of the European lenders from my foreign aid and embassy days, and I knew they have money to spend, but that they were slow, bureaucratic, and normally linked their loan to procurement in their home country. I went to the Chinese development bank and was told that their minimum loans started at 500 million USD. So, I aimed for the two largest national development financing companies. After meetings and presentations of project information memorandums, and with the equity commitment letters in place, they agreed to look at the possibility of them joining as lenders. And then they started their due diligence process. And this is where project finance really becomes tricky.

Risk identification and allocation is a key component in project finance. The financial lenders, and their due diligence teams, shall conclude if the risks inherent in project development, construction, and operation are too high, making the project unfinanceable. This makes the lenders' due diligence process complicated, intense, and often confusing. My project became the subject of numerous technical, environmental, economic, and political risk assessment teams from the lenders. Our construction, supply, offtake, and concession contracts and agreements were scrutinized. Risks, the sales pricing methodology, pricing of assets, the financial model, joint-ownership structures, deal structure, the associated collaterals and guarantees, EPC and equipment suppliers guarantees, performance guarantees, offtake guarantees, and so on were identified, documented, scrutinized, and evaluated. Not once, but many times. The lenders changed teams, or reorganized, and we had to start again. And months passed. The slow process then created validity period overruns for the documents I had provided. Fluctuation in the exchange rate meant the supply contracts had to be redone. Offtake agreements had to be updated.

That South Africa only had a few large-scale biogas facilities and that several projects had failed in the past did not make the due diligence process easier. The funders had not approved funding for a biogas facility in the last many years and this was the first time they had a bio-CNG project for loan and due diligence consideration. The funding officials and their due diligence teams were on their toes, their bosses skeptical. This meant that the lenders would not go alone but required to have at least two lenders on board. This meant that different debt instruments were to be used, and it became difficult to agree upon which actors should get priority in case of default. Detailed analysis of the different shareholder agreements, the loan agreements, and the legal regulation now had to be undertaken to understand the situation clearly. More time passed.

And I used months after months behind the screen. The amount of documentation required by the lenders was next-level stuff. At the final submission, it amounted to 76 documents, 425 pages. My many years of writing technical reports, legal document, proposals, and presentations had made me a quick writer. At least there we won some time. And we got through it all, not on time, but we got there. Due diligence approved, followed by commitment letters from the lenders.

I learned to expect the unforeseen. One reason IPP project developments take so long is all the unforeseen stuff. We had been having very good meetings with one of the most reputable and successful equity funders in the country, and they had signed the letter of joint equity funding which I could take to the lenders. That was at the same time I had two community agro-villages projects running. To make a long story short, one of the community board members hung me out to dry in the media, the equity funder saw it, and they canceled our cooperation then and there. Nine months lost and back to the drawing board. Finding equity funders to partner with is difficult. Now it became double difficult. But the world is big, and stubbornness helps. Another equity partner came on board. And I could again continue with the lenders that were on board but had been put in a waiting position. We went through and passed their due diligence with several CPs (condition precedent, a term in project finance I got to know very well). Then one of the lenders made changes in the leadership, and the new management team decided that they would not approve loans with CPs anymore. Reasonable, but it hit my project. One of my CPs was the EIA approval, which had proven, for reasons difficult to understand, hard to get out of the Environment Department. And months passed waiting for the EIA approval to arrive. And then the deadline for the due diligence approval lapsed, and the lender withdrew their loan offer, but said I could submit again as a new project when the EIA had arrived. They would try to fast track, but it had to be treated as a new submission. Back to square one.

The EIA approval took over two years to get. This was a green project, producing green fuel in a green ecosystem circular way, no chemicals, no waste, everything the world wants. And everything an Environment Department should support. Not so. One nonrelevant question after another, one public hearing after another, new environment officers, new heads of department, new regulations, new requirements—I felt two decades had stood still, I was back in Borneo and again working with the stupid environmental impact assessment system. It was tough to handle, but, with government officers, we learn to bow our head. And wait. And wait. And one day, the approval will come.

The last of the unforeseens that hit not only my project, but the world was the COVID pandemic. The virus came, offices closed, officers went home, and more project development time passed. Not much to do about that, just another unforeseen thing that contributed to increasing the length of the project development period.

I learned that it can be tricky to plan the project development process. The development sequence became not nearly as straightforward as I had thought and planned. Normally, with IPP energy business planning, the sequence is first to gain technical skills and expertise (to know what you are talking about), find a buyer (to pull the train), then find the right inputs and technology (to maximize the business case), and when you have these platforms, find the money (to make it happen). All key, but maybe the buyer most so. We can have expertise, inputs, and even money, but without a buyer, we go nowhere with a business plan.

We first developed a *technical platform* correctly through practical technical experience with feasibility, design, construction, and operation of biogas facilities. We did this in cooperation with a strong international biogas technology partner. All good and fine. Based on this, we were able to find a *buyer platform* through partnering for CNG offtake. Also, as it should be. But then we had to detour to get to the input platform. Peet and I visited several of the biggest feedstock suppliers in the country, the large chicken consortia and the large cattle farmers, some with more than 150,000 cattle. Good meetings, but we knew we got nowhere. To lock in a feedstock supplier became a real problem. The chicken consortia were going alone with their energy production based on their waste and balance sheets and did not need an IPP. The large cattle and maize farmers were old generational family-owned farmers—tough, hardworking, successful, and very busy and strangely difficult to find. They run business with turnover of hundreds of millions but are invisible. They are not on Google, have no homepage, and do not advertise. They operate in closed circles. I knew we had to approach this differently. I called my accountant Fannie that had his business in the agricultural Free State. He is a good accountant and very likable. I knew he had thousands of clients, and some of them had to be farmers. They were, and he linked me up with Geoffrey, and with him I toured the provinces in the agricultural heartland for almost a year. Geoffrey is a go-getter, a talker, and he talks Afrikaans. He established meetings with more than 20 large-scale farmers; we went, had coffee, and talked farming. And we learned. We learned technical farming and manure stuff, pricing, timing, and quantities. And we learned that they did not really need us or a biogas project. They are rich and busy and already managed and made money on their manure.

We learned that farmers are risk-averse when it comes to new areas outside their experience. And they should be. They had heard about the failing biogas facilities in South Africa; they had heard and read about the biogas industry in Europe but had never seen a successful one. Most of them said, let us see some good operational facilities and then we will join. And all asked if we had signed contracts with the CNG buyer and the funders. They wanted to see our buyer and our money first. Experienced business-people I thought. We had the buyer, but not the money as we needed a signed feedstock supply contract to move to the funding platform.

Luckily, a few of them had mercy on us, probably thinking let us give them a chance and see what happens, as long as we do not have to use time or money on it. Handshakes were made. Simple supply terms were signed, without being read, as they all said, this is our hood (not in those words), we have agreed on pricing, so a handshake is sufficient. To get to these supply term sheets proved to be surprisingly hard and took much more time than I had expected. But now I at least had simple but signed supply term sheets, and I could approach equity funders and lenders for project finance, and the *funding platform* slowly fell in place. Now I was finally able to convincingly go back to the large farmers to sign input agreements and complete the *feedstock supply platform*.

Through all this, I learned the importance of each platform, that there is a back-and-forth oscillation between them before they fall in place, and that we are nowhere before all four platforms are present and signed. I learned that it takes considerable effort and time, and that when we are entrepreneurs, we must keep moving forward. We unavoidably hit walls, become dizzy, but must be able to shake it off, back off a step or two, reorient, go a bit to the side, and then move with full speed ahead again—until we hit a new wall and must repeat the procedure.

I learned that to charge and spin is all that matters and having the ability to evolve, differentiate, and cooperate is what makes us spin. I do not know whether I will succeed in the IPP PPA sector as an individual bio-CNG entrepreneur, but I am close. Next year? I think so. Hope so. At least this attempt took me out of foreign aid, out of nonsensical EIA work (almost), out of wicked rural development contexts, and back to spinning with rational technical issues and people in a sector that makes sense and where I can concentrate my energy on juggling the four issues of technical, people, power, and the unforeseen. How nice would it be if we could just select a strategy, put all our energy and efforts into this one strategy, and then be successful. And how easy would it be if the only skill required was the ability to fight and outcompete competitors. That, however, is not how it works or plays out.

Will I become an asset owner? Will I spin off five bio-CNG SPVs after five years and become rich? It does not matter. And I mean it because my consultancy and project management platforms sustain me and I will be fine. Through my attempt to get to the third ladder, I met good professionals, upgraded my skills, and realized how closely the story of not only my entrepreneurial years but my professional life also has been linked to Darwin's discovery that development of all life happens through variation, differentiation, and cooperation.

CHAPTER 6

The Future Anchors

I have tried to give a guided tour to the realities of our individual professional life. Our professionalism is anchored in a profession, in my case project management, and, from thereon, is a mixed bungle of experiences, technical skills, work contexts, change, problems, balances, cooperation and competition, failure, learning and knowledge, logic, innovations, rationality, success and motivation, empathy, power and conflicts, constraints and creativity, time, happiness, and maturing.

It should be clear by now that our technical skills are only but one of several skills we need to acquire to become good project managers and good professionals. The experience and context matrix provide a mental model for other equally important skills we need to acquire and continuously update to climb up the professional capacity levels.

To become professional project managers, we must continuously feed our brain with experiences, reference points, and mental models. We must learn and develop mental models from the few, from projects we have been engulfed in long enough to get specific, deep, and detailed contextual knowledge. And we must learn from the many, from our accumulated normal experiences and reference points, to see patterns and learn from these normal accumulations, and try not to lean too heavily on the few outliers or failures. We must continuously add other professionals' reference points and professional stories to our own experiences to acquire further width and variation. And we must continuously update and upgrade our mental models from the really many, from big data and big picture contexts we cannot get a hold of from our own small experience-based point of view.

We need to continuously feed our brain with all these, so the brain can do its spreading activation thing and make us think and behave professionally. The neurons and electrical circuits must fire.

Our individual professional capacity is networked and evolutionary—mine, yours, everyone's. Evolution means incremental and gradual change. Evolution means cumulative change from simple beginnings. Evolution follows a narrative, from one stage to the next; it creeps rather than jumps. Evolution is the way to understand how our professional capacities changes and evolves by gradual, incremental emergent changes driven by selection among competing experiences and mental models.

Collectively, the situation is the same but different. Our collective professional achievements are also entirely a networking phenomenon. It is by putting brains together through the division of labor and specialization, trade and globalization, through AI and the Internet, that we stumbled upon ways to raise our professional capacities, living standards, technological virtuosity, and common knowledge. Our big picture achievements are based on collective intelligence and accumulated combined professional capacities. By each doing one thing and getting good at it, then sharing and combining the results through exchange and networks, we become capable of doing things we do not even understand.[1] The strength of our collective professional networks is one of the most critical and complex forces ever released on Earth.

I think that what we have to draw our attention to in this century is our collective professional networks, our common distributed networks, and how we make these work better for us all. Read any of John Brockman's Edge.org books[2] and be inspired to come to the same conclusion. Biological, human, organizational, and societal realities are distributed networks. Complex environments are networks. Computers are networked. Epidemics are networks. Business relations are networked. Families are networks. Politics are networked. Professional relations too. The workings of professional distributed networks are what we jointly have to get a better hold on in this century.

If we have 10 professionals in a group, there are a maximum of 45 possible connections between them. If we increase the number of professionals to 1,000, the number of possible ties increases to 499,500. So, when the number of professionals increases by 100-fold, the number of possible professional ties increases more than 10,000-fold.[3] The demographic explosion will make the global population go from 1 billion to 10 billion in just two centuries and this will fundamentally change our human distributed networks. The professional middle class, which today is half the world's population, will reach around eight billion at the end of the century, and this will make our human distributed network primarily a distributed network between professionals: 150,000 new professional middle classers will enter the global pool of professionals *every day* for the next 75 years. That is a lot of new professionals, and a lot of new project managers.

As we continue to network the world, complexity grows faster, and many aspects of our professional world become emergent and nonpredictable. These ever-larger distributed networks provide us with professional working contexts where processes increasingly will become bottom-up, self-organized, self-generated, and self-guided. Our economy is a self-organized bottom-up emergent process of professionals just trying to make a living. In big networked systems, there are no overriding big plans or top-down strategic planning, no apparent system or method but primarily small steps, processes, and interactions that make up the context. Achievements and progress here happen through our own self-organized professional processes mixed up with others' self-organized professional processes.

Unfortunately, understanding large-scale distributed networks does not come naturally.[4] It is an appreciation not of the simple but of the complex. Unlike induction or empiricism, our big picture distributed professional networked context takes effort, slow thinking, spreading activation, experience, and exposure to acquire and appreciate. Distributed networks and bottom-up reasoning are counterintuitive. Our brains evolved to find structure and mental models to understand the little world that surrounds us, and we intuitively sense that anything that looks to have a structure must have received this structure from the top down, not bottom up. Many still see the world from the top down and believe that economies must be designed and that countries and the world should be ruled or managed from the top down.

Still, for the past 500 years, we have gradually transitioned from top-down to bottom-up systems. From kings, strong men, and dictators to democracies and time-restricted politicians. And, from there, hopefully to even more bottom-up loose-coupled methods for running our societal and professional life. Switzerland with its yearly rotating state leadership is on to something. We must stop talking about leaders in complex distributed networks; we must stop thinking and talking of politicians or professionals running a mega-city, a province, a country, or a multinational company. Such large-scale entities are never run by persons; they are distributed networked systems with a dynamism and self-emergent development outside the control of one, two, or any number of specified group of leaders or professionals. In all complex distributed networked settings, we need to get rid of our fascination with leaders, managers, and management systems. We need to be at ease with not knowing how the complex systems we participate in are controlled or developed. To make this point personal, in the era where I have become a professional globalist, in an era with rapid globalization, urbanization, mega-cities, and atomization, I have experienced a fast-decreasing interest in the need to know which king, minister, or leader is pretending to run the place I am working in. I do not need to know their names and do not want to know the details of their self-indulgent and simple tinkering and power plays for them to stay wealthy and privileged. I need them to get out of my way.

Professionalism in large-scale networked systems is the result of millions of professionals exchanging and sharing professional knowledge. By enabling us to work for and with each other, we steadily become more specialized and professional in what we jointly know and produce. Distributed bottom-up networks linking millions of professionals, and project managers, will be a key theme for this century. Knowledge will become more and more collective; innovation and growth will become more bottom up; and large corporations, political parties, and government bureaucracies will diminish and fragment. This will not go smoothly or without resistance, but I think and hope it will happen.

For it to happen, we need to improve the ability of professionals, organizations, and societies to make collective networked decisions with intelligence greater than the individual.[5] This can be accomplished in small groups of professionals through conversation, but the method does not scale well. For larger groups, the state-of-the-art method for collective decision making is still the vote. Voting only works to the degree that, on average, each voter can individually determine the right decision.

That is not good enough. We need to sort out how to right size our political, organizational, and professional decision-making systems. And we need to *increase our understanding of distributed networks.* We need to understand the spread of truth and lies, political stances and viruses, and wealth and poverty reduction in distributed networks.[6] And in all fields, we need more topology and metrics that recognize the mesh of networked connections. Peer-to-peer, density, centrality, betweenness, multiplexity, reciprocity, bridging, bonding, network effects, and strength of ties are distributed network concepts and mental models we need to become much more comfortable with.[7] We need to utilize the power of visual imagery better, as the visual makes complex connections, natural systems, urban expansions, and dynamic networks in process much more vivid. Written text works brilliantly, but the marriage of the written and the visual provide us with new ways to understand and present complex distributed networked connections.[8]

In this century, we all need to focus much more on how distributed professional networks can bring us further. If I started out today, I would choose to be one of the professionals that got fully emerged in projects that focused on the development and fine-tuning of collective distributed professional networks. As a professional, however, I would *continue to be a pragmatic gradualist.*[9] I would continue to highly value gradual and evolutionary developments in politics and professional life and decision making. I would not want to see radical change dictated from the top; I would not want to see ideologies; and I would not want to see quick solutions. I would want to see slow, messy, compromised, unglamorous, bureaucratic but professional endless negotiated small improvements. I would want to see us try to do a half-decent job for as many people as possible, trying to set things up a little better for the future. I am not sure I want to see politicians. I would continue to accept and appreciate that professionals who are experts in their field tend to be skeptical, even cynical, of experimental claims that contradict the commonly accepted knowledge, not because they are hopelessly encumbered by tradition but because that knowledge has passed a startlingly diverse array of professional tests. I would continue to fight false biases and wrong mental models entering my reasoning.

The next professional me would be able to speak and write Chinese Mandarin, be called

卡斯滕·霍兰德·劳格森,

and because I know my brain likes lists, I would continue to update a list of professional and personal rules for nobody but me:

- Count my professional experiences as these are the most valuable things I own.
- Read good books, some of them too complicated to understand; just lean back and know something will accumulate.
- Mass, charge, spin, that's the purpose of it all.
- Continue to practice and improve my professional juggling skills.
- Trust and look people in the eye.
- Never steal or lie.
- Give people a second chance but not a third (if about money, no second chance).
- Bring my favorite music into each day.
- Choose my life partner carefully. From this one decision comes so much of our happiness and misery.
- Do not burn bridges.
- Remember that a quarter of my success is based on my ability to deal with people, a quarter on my technical skills, a quarter on my ability to play the power game, and a quarter on luck.
- Remember, no one makes it alone.
- Always side with the global poor.
- Professionals are only professionals when I think they are.
- Always focus on the how-to.
- Take the scenic route.
- Know my illusions of explanatory depth.
- Be a pragmatic gradualist.
- Answer the phone with enthusiasm and energy.
- Define success.

- Show respect for everyone who works for a living, regardless of what they do.
- Repetitive normality is King.
- Be modest. Many have accomplished more than me.
- Give. Think of the reason later.
- Do not get overwhelmed by the chaos variation brings.
- Do not expect life to be fair.

Platforms

As this book is about professional capacity, and as professional capacity is individually held based on our own accumulated experiences and reference points, it is only appropriate to be transparent about the professional and private me. I have uploaded on my homepage my full CV with contact persons and phone numbers for each of my 225 projects, a list of my professional network, and my publication list.[1] As you will see, my career has been good but not exceptional. I have had a normal professional global career, and this is good as it makes my project management and professional experiences and lessons learned relevant not for the few or aspiring billionaires of this world, but for the around three billion normal middle-class professionals roaming around.

The general inspirations and references for the book are my projects, the people in my professional network, and the books I have read. You can find a list of the books that has given me professional and private reference points on my homepage,[2] which is chosen among the books I have in my library. I pulled out a book and asked if this was a good book. For most, I could not remember the story or the specific content, but something in my memory always said no or yes, this was a good inspiring book.

Of the books I have read, I only keep the books I like. The list on my homepage includes the books that have taught and inspired me most, all kept neatly in alphabetic order in my small library. Books have followed me all my life. They have given me life or, as more eloquently formulated by Richard Dawkins, books do furnish a life. And the books in my library have traveled. They have followed me everywhere. Some of them started out in Aalborg, Denmark, in 1980, then traveled with me to Copenhagen where more was added, then we all moved around the world to Kota Kinabalu on Borneo, and from there to Bangkok, Thailand. Then they moved with me back to Copenhagen, and finally now have ended up in Johannesburg, South Africa. Some of them look a bit tired and maybe, just maybe, this is where they will end up.

I have 748 books in my library, half of them fiction, the other half nonfiction. I recon I keep every second book I read, which means that I have read something like 1,496 books, or 37.4 books per year or 3.1 books per month for 40 years. Useless statistics for nobody but myself, but sometimes it is fun to play with numbers. And another useless fact would show that the nonfiction books I like are anchored in biology, physics, organizations, strategy, economy, evolution, and history, and the fiction books are grouped into three types—books with a good storyline: Boyd, Torday, and Towles all tell straightforward and very readable stories; slightly surreal books: Pinol, Yanagihara, Buzatti, and Martel all blow my mind; and books located in, for me, an exotic setting: Hansen, Stangerup, Conrad, Butler, Roberts, and Mistry all take me to places where my mind can wander.

Notes

Why Experience Matters

1. www.carstenhlaugesen.com.

Chapter 1

1. Saunders (2011).
2. Kharas (2017).
3. Canals (2019).

Chapter 2

1. Dreyfus and Dreyfus (1980).
2. Ibid.
3. Rosen (2012), pp. 203–205.
4. Mukherjee (2016).
5. Pinker (2003).
6. Minda (2021).

Chapter 3

1. www.carstenhlaugesen.com.
2. www.carstenhlaugesen.com.
3. Wilczek (2021).
4. Deutsch (2011).
5. Schank (2018), pp. 363–364.

Chapter 4

1. Koch (2020).
2. Nørretranders (2012), pp. 226–228.
3. Waytz (2018), pp. 6–7.
4. Wikipedia (n.d.).

5. www.carstenhlaugesen.com.
6. Norvig (2018), pp. 106–107.
7. Devlin (2018), pp. 110–112.
8. Shostak (2018), pp. 113–114.
9. Shirky (2012), pp. 198–200.
10. Giussani (2018), pp. 115–117.
11. O'Donnell (2018), pp. 271–272.
12. Pinol (2008).
13. Conrad (1902).
14. Jordison (2015).
15. Laugesen, Brix, Koottatep, and Fryd (2010).
16. Ibid.
17. Ibid.

Chapter 5

1. Mintzberg (1992).
2. Baldwin (2016).
3. Morland (2019).
4. Darwin (2011).
5. Koch (2020).
6. Ibid.
7. Ibid.

Chapter 6

1. Ridley (2012), pp. 257–258.
2. Brockman (n.d.).
3. Christakis (2012), pp. 81–83.
4. Scott (2010).
5. Hillis (2010), pp. 22–35.
6. Shermer (2012), pp. 157–159.
7. Rafaeli (2018), pp. 399–403.
8. Wyatt (2017), pp. 546–549.
9. Eno (2009), pp. 282–284.

Platforms

1. www.carstenhlaugesen.com.
2. Ibid.

References

Baldwin, R. 2016. *The Great Convergence*. Belknap Harvard.

Brockman, J. n.d. *Edge.Org*. HarperCollins.

Canals, C. 2019. *The Emergence of the Middle Class*. Caisa Bank Research.

Christakis, N.A. 2012. "Holism." In *This Will Make You Smarter*, ed. J. Brockman, 81–83. HarperCollins.

Conrad, J. 1902. *Heart of Darkness*. Penguin Books.

Darwin, C. 2011. *The Origin of Species*. Harper Press.

Deutsch, D. 2011. *The Beginning of Infinity*. Allan Lane.

Devlin, K. 2018. "Number Sense." In *This Idea Is Brilliant*, ed. J. Brockman, 110–112. HarperCollins.

Dreyfus, S.E. and H.L. Dreyfus. 1980. *A Five-Stage Model of the Mental Activities Involved in Directed Skill Acquisition*. California Univ Berkeley Operations Research Center.

Eno, B. 2009. "From Revolutionary to Evolutionary." In *What Have You Changed Your Mind About*, ed. J. Brockman, 282–284. HarperCollins.

Giussani, B. 2018. "Exponential." In *This Idea Is Brilliant*, ed. J. Brockman, 115–117. HarperCollins.

Hillis, W.D. 2010. "A Forebrain for the World Brain." In *This Will Change Everything*, ed. J. Brockman, 22–35. HarperCollins.

Jordison, S. July 29, 2015. "Heart of Darkness by Joseph Conrad." *Guardian*.

Kharas, H. 2017. "The Unprecedented Expansion of the Global Middle Class." *Global Economy and Development working paper 100*. Brookings.

Koch, R. 2020. *Beyond the 80/20 Principle*. Nicolas Brealey Press.

Laugesen, C.H., H. Brix, T. Koottatep, and O. Fryd. 2010. *Sustainable Wastewater Management in Developing Countries*. ASCE Press.

Minda, J.P. 2021. *How to Think*. Robinson.

Mintzberg, H. 1992. *Structures in 5*. Pearson.

Morland, P. 2019. *The Human Tide*. John Murray Press.

Mukherjee, S. 2016. *The Gene*. Bodley Head.

Nørretranders, T. 2012. "Depth." In *This Will Make You Smarter*, ed. J. Brockman, 226–228. HarperCollins.

Norvig, P. 2018. "Counting." In *This Idea Is Brilliant*, ed. J. Brockman, 106–107. HarperCollins.

O'Donnell, J.J. 2018. "Regression to the Mean." In *This Idea Is Brilliant*, ed. J. Brockman, 271–272. HarperCollins.

Pinker, S. 2003. *The Blank Slate*. Penguin Books.

Pinol, A.S. 2008. *Pandora in the Congo*. Canongate Books.

Rafaeli, S. 2018. "Networks." In *This Idea Is Brilliant*, ed. J. Brockman, 399–403. HarperCollins.

Ridley, S. 2012. "Collective Intelligence." In *This Will Make You Smarter*, ed. J. Brockman, 257–258. HarperCollins.

Rosen, J. 2012. "Wicked Problems." In *This Will Make You Smarter*, ed. J. Brockman, 203–205. HarperCollins.

Saunders, D. 2011. *Arrival City*. Windmill Books.

Schank, R. 2018. "Case-Based Reasoning." In *This Idea Is Brilliant*, ed. J. Brockman, 363–364. HarperCollins.

Scott, R. 2010. *The Rational Optimist*. Fourth Estate.

Shermer, M. 2012. "Think Bttom Up, Not Top Down." In *This Will Make You Smarter*, ed. J. Brockman, 157–159. HarperCollins.

Shirky, C. 2012. "The Pareto Principle." In *This Will Make You Smarter*, ed. J. Brockman, 198–200. HarperCollins.

Shostak, S. 2018. "Fermi Problems." In *This Idea Is Brilliant*, ed. J. Brockman, 113–114. HarperCollins.

Waytz, A. 2018. "The Illusion of Explanatory Depth." In *This Idea Is Brilliant*, ed. J. Brockman, 6–7. HarperCollins.

Wikipedia. n.d. "Profession."

Wilczek, F. 2021. *Fundamentals, Ten Keys to Reality*. Allen Lane.

www.carstenhlaugesen.com.

Wyatt, V. 2017. "The Convergence of Images and Technology." In *Know This*, ed. J. Brockman, 546–549. HarperCollins.

About the Author

Carsten H. Laugesen has, for the last three decades, been project manager, project developer, program manager, chief technical advisor, technical expert, and team leader for 225 projects worldwide. He has worked in the Danish Government, in one of the largest European engineering consultancy companies, in the Ministry of Foreign Affairs as a diplomat, and in the last decade in South Africa as a successful entrepreneur and company owner. He has worked in 24 countries, authored 11 books, published 22 articles, adopted 7 policies and laws, and written 584 client-approved technical reports. His expertise and publications cover project management, program development, evaluation, capacity development, renewable energy, energy efficiency, private sector development, development assistance, rural development, appropriate wastewater management, quality assurance, management by objectives, and health care management. He lives in Johannesburg with his wife and five dogs.

Index

OTHER TITLES IN THE PORTFOLIO AND PROJECT MANAGEMENT COLLECTION

Kam Jugdev, Athabasca University, Editor

- *Power Skills That Lead to Exceptional Performance* by Neal Whitten
- *A Project Sponsor's Warp-Speed Guide* by Yogi Schulz and Jocelyn Lapointe
- *Great Meetings Build Great Teams* by Rich Maltzman and Jim Stewart
- *When Graduation's Over, Learning Begins* by Roger Forsgren
- *Project Control Methods and Best Practices* by Yakubu Olawale
- *Managing Projects With PMBOK 7* by James W. Marion and Tracey Richardson
- *Shields Up* by Gregory J. Skulmoski
- *Greatness in Construction History* by Sherif Hashem
- *The Inner Building Blocks* by Abhishek Rai
- *Project Profitability* by Reginald Tomas Lee
- *Moving the Needle With Lean OKRs* by Bart den Haak
- *Lean Knowledge Management* by Roger Forsgren

Concise and Applied Business Books

The Collection listed above is one of 30 business subject collections that Business Expert Press has grown to make BEP a premiere publisher of print and digital books. Our concise and applied books are for...

- Professionals and Practitioners
- Faculty who adopt our books for courses
- Librarians who know that BEP's Digital Libraries are a unique way to offer students ebooks to download, not restricted with any digital rights management
- Executive Training Course Leaders
- Business Seminar Organizers

Business Expert Press books are for anyone who needs to dig deeper on business ideas, goals, and solutions to everyday problems. Whether one print book, one ebook, or buying a digital library of 110 ebooks, we remain the affordable and smart way to be business smart. For more information, please visit www.businessexpertpress.com, or contact sales@businessexpertpress.com.

www.ingramcontent.com/pod-product-compliance
Lightning Source LLC
Chambersburg PA
CBHW061308220326
41599CB00026B/4786